D0223072

African Arguments

Written by experts with an unrivalled knowledge of the
continent, African Arguments is a series of concise, engaging
books that address the key issues currently facing Africa.
Topical and thought-provoking, accessible but in-depth, they
provide essential reading for anyone interested in getting to
the heart of both why contemporary Africa is the way it is
and how it is changing.

African Arguments Online

African Arguments Online is a website managed by the
Royal African Society, which hosts debates on the African
Arguments series and other topical issues that affect Africa:
http://africanarguments.org

Titles already published

Forthcoming

Published by Zed Books with the support of the following organizations:

International African Institute promotes scholarly understanding of Africa, notably its changing societies, cultures and languages. Founded in 1926 and based in London, it supports a range of seminars and publications including the journal *Africa*.

www.internationalafricaninstitute.org

Royal African Society is Britain's prime Africa organization. Now more than a hundred years old, its in-depth, long-term knowledge of the continent and its peoples makes the Society the first stop for anyone wishing to know more about the continent. RAS fosters a better understanding of Africa in the UK and throughout the world – its history, politics, culture, problems and potential. RAS disseminates this knowledge and insight and celebrates the diversity and depth of African culture.

www.royalafricansociety.org

World Peace Foundation, founded in 1910, is located at the Fletcher School, Tufts University. The Foundation's mission is to promote innovative research and teaching, believing that these are critical to the challenges of making peace around the world, and should go hand in hand with advocacy and practical engagement with the toughest issues. Its central theme is 'reinventing peace' for the twenty-first century.

www.worldpeacefoundation.org

About the authors

Neil Carrier is a researcher based at the African Studies Centre, Oxford. He has published widely on the substance khat, which he first studied in Kenya and in the UK for his PhD in social anthropology at the University of St Andrews (2004). In recent years, Carrier's focus has broadened to drugs in Africa more generally, and he has also carried out research in East Africa on a range of other issues, from film and photography to indigeneity. His current project focuses on the Somali diaspora and their impact upon Eastleigh, a Nairobi estate recently transformed into a booming commercial zone.

Gernot Klantschnig is assistant professor in international studies at the University of Nottingham, Ningbo, China. He completed his DPhil in politics at St Antony's College, Oxford in 2008. His doctoral research, which is to be published as *Drugs, Crime and the State in Africa: The Nigerian Connection*, examined Nigeria's role in the international trade and control of illegal drugs. His recent research and publications have also focused on the international politics of crime control, West African law enforcement, as well as China's growing economic and political engagement with Africa.

NEIL CARRIER AND
GERNOT KLANTSCHNIG

Africa and the war on drugs

Zed Books
LONDON | NEW YORK

in association with

International African Institute
Royal African Society
World Peace Foundation

Africa and the war on drugs was first published in association with the International African Institute, the Royal African Society and the World Peace Foundation in 2012 by Zed Books Ltd, 7 Cynthia Street, London N1 9JF, UK and Room 400, 175 Fifth Avenue, New York, NY 10010, USA

www.zedbooks.co.uk
www.internationalafricaninstitute.org
www.royalafricansociety.org
www.worldpeacefoundation.org

Set in OurType Arnhem and Futura Bold by
Ewan Smith, London
Cover design: www.roguefour.co.uk
Index: ed.emery@thefreeuniversity.net
Printed and bound by CPI Group (UK) Ltd, Croydon,
CRO 4YY

Distributed in the USA exclusively by Palgrave Macmillan, a division of St Martin's Press, LLC, 175 Fifth Avenue, New York, NY 10010, USA.

A catalogue record for this book is available from the British Library
US CIP data are available from the Library of Congress

ISBN 978 1 84813 967 1 hb
ISBN 978 1 84813 966 4 pb

Contents

Introduction

We've been fighting the drugs war for 30 years – now a new front has opened up. (Veteran international police official)[1]

We are united in our understanding about the threat drug trafficking poses to Africa and to US interests, and why we must collectively boost our coordination and efforts now to prevent a tidal wave of addictions, drug-related enterprises, corruption, instability and conflict from overwhelming Africa's shores. (Johnnie Carson, US Assistant Secretary of State for African Affairs)[2]

Why Africa? Why now?

According to a recent flurry of official statements, UN reports, Wikileaks cables and newspaper articles, African countries are facing an increasingly grave threat. This is not from the HIV/AIDS epidemic, nor from ongoing conflict, terrorism or corruption – though these are connected – but instead from a plague that previously seemed to have spared Africa its worst depredations: drugs. From 'narco-states' in West Africa to accounts of 'teens frenzied in drug abuse' in the East, the standard drugs rhetoric of the West and its media is being vociferously applied to a continent previously low down the priority list of international policymakers. Africa is said to be imperilled by an 'invisible tide' of drug trafficking and abuse, and several African countries declare themselves at 'crisis point' and declare drug abuse to be a 'national disaster'.

Much of the recent international concern has focused on West Africa and its role as a transhipment point for South American cocaine destined for Europe, and the fear that countries such as Guinea-Bissau are transforming into 'narco-states'. However, concerns about drugs have been increasing throughout the continent as the perception grows that drug production, trade and use are all rising steeply and that drugs will mire Africans in underdevelopment and consequent poverty. This book seeks to appraise this talk of 'crisis points' and 'national disasters' by examining the history and contemporary situation regarding Sub-Saharan Africa and drugs. The war on drugs, we will argue, has led to much sensationalizing of the drug situation in Africa, and has been decidedly counterproductive in dealing with the real problems surrounding the production, trade and use of drugs, leading to repressive policies, increased corruption and violation of human rights. Of course, this is a familiar story from other regions targeted by the war on drugs, and we argue that the emphasis on increased law enforcement and talk of 'drug-free societies' has sidelined discussions on human rights in drug policy, the provision of drug treatment facilities and a focus on more pressing drug issues for Africans, including that of the trade in fake medicines. The war on drugs in Africa is at heart an initiative driven by western interests; it is time to examine the issues from the point of view of Africa.

Over the course of the next four chapters, we show how many of the drugs consumed, traded and produced on the continent are more embedded in African societies than commonly assumed. The book describes how the indigenous (khat), the ubiquitous (cannabis) and the recently introduced (heroin, cocaine, methamphetamine) affect African societies, providing threats to consumers, but also providing opportunities to producers and entrepreneurs. We also explore how various African countries have sought to address this issue, usually through the importation of supply control measures that are highly repressive in nature, and highlight the policy alternatives that rarely get acknowledged or sufficient funding in the African context.

The global war on drugs

Internationally, the war on drugs has come to be especially associated with the USA, and the phrase itself was first promoted by Richard Nixon in 1972 who declared 'total war' on 'America's public enemy number one', that is to say, drugs.[3] The USA has certainly been a prime mover in global drug policy, pushing an agenda of prohibition and harsh supply-reduction measures that in their militarized form truly resemble a war. However, we do not restrict our use of the term purely to US policy, instead using it as a trope for both prohibitionist policy towards drugs in general, and for a hegemonic way of thinking about various substances labelled as 'drugs'.

Policy and institutions Drugs were not always dealt with through the prohibition prescribed by the drugs war. Before the twentieth century, free trade had been the guiding norm of the international commerce in drugs. The Opium Wars were to change all that, propelling the issue of drug policy to the fore of international debates. The first treaty restricting the trade of opium in Asia was signed between the British and Chinese governments in 1907 and two years later diplomats from all over the world met at the Shanghai Opium Commission to discuss the globalization of this system of control. In subsequent years China and the US government spearheaded international control measures in the face of opposition from the main drug producing, manufacturing and trading states, resulting in the 1912 Hague International Opium Convention, the first international treaty of drug control. Initial concern with opium soon broadened to include cocaine and also cannabis and, interestingly, the inclusion of the latter substance was driven by governments on the African continent – by a 1923 request from the South African colonial government and a subsequent recommendation by Egypt.[4] By the 1930s a series of multilateral conferences and conventions had established a system to restrict the manufacture, trade and use of opium, coca, cannabis and their derivatives solely to 'medical and scientific use'.[5] While initially successful in curbing the trade in these drugs, in the years following the Second World War the illegal trade in these substances grew quickly. In response, new treaties were negotiated to control the illegal side of the drug trade, and the

3

Single Convention on Narcotic Drugs, signed in 1961, was the culmination of this international effort.

This convention remains the principal and most universally accepted international law on drug control. While it aims to ensure adequate medical and scientific supply of opium, coca and cannabis products, the convention also strictly prohibits all other cultivation, manufacture, trade and use of these drugs. Most states today use a licensing system for transactions in domestic drug markets and report their use, trade and manufacture of medically used opiates, cocaine and cannabis to a UN body called the International Narcotics Control Board (INCB). This system tightly regulates all legal use of controlled substances, while prohibiting and criminalizing their trade and manufacture for non-medical uses.

International drug policies that followed the 1961 convention confirmed its dominant ideas on criminal justice-oriented drug control.[6] The second major international convention still in force today, the 1988 Convention Against Illicit Traffic in Narcotic Drugs and Psychotropic Substances, was a direct outcome of President Reagan's war on drugs in the second half of the 1980s and aimed to strengthen international cooperation in the field of policing, prosecution and punishment of drug offences. This law enforcement emphasis essentially means a reinforcement of drug supply control methods at the cost of alternative methods from the medical, educational and development fields. The signing of this convention was strongly supported by the majority of African governments at the time, although the lack of its full implementation in African countries has been a major concern for the INCB ever since 1988.

The legal system to control the global drug trade is backed up by a range of international and national drug agencies that promote its values and its implementation. Aside from the INCB, a variety of other UN bodies have made sure that government policies are in line with the prohibitionist ideas of the conventions. The UN Office on Drugs and Crime (UNODC), headquartered in Vienna and with a network of field offices including some in Africa, is the centre of the UN drug bureaucracy. Like the INCB, the UNODC monitors and lobbies member states, but it also conducts its own research and technical assistance projects in developing countries, especially in drug hotspots in Latin America and Central Asia and increasingly in Africa. While the INCB has shown unwavering support for the supply control and law enforcement focused legal regime, elements of the UNODC have considered alternative ideas on drug control, such as 'harm reduction' (see below). However, as the UNODC is greatly dependent on funding from major donor countries, above all the US, Sweden and Japan, its work has had to follow their law enforcement-oriented interests. Even in the UNODC's own words, one of the bureaucracy's weaknesses is to have 'shown an instinct for repressive rather than preventive operations'.[7]

In addition, national agencies have always coexisted with these UN drug bodies and some of them have replicated the UN with a similarly wide range of international activities. While specialized national drug agencies have only started to appear in Africa in recent years, the highly influential US Drug Enforcement Administration (DEA) has had a network of 'special agents' in most countries of interest to US supply control for decades. In states such as Colombia and Bolivia these agents have been present in the dozens and at times led whole drug war campaigns. Many of these DEA operations have caused local resentment against breaches of national laws and sovereignty, and some countries have subsequently banned these US drug warriors.[8] While their presence in Africa has been less significant, the number of special agents across the continent has grown considerably in recent years, as will be illustrated later on. As these DEA agents primarily focus on the global interdiction of drugs, they act as a global police force ensuring the international prohibition of drugs.

Rhetoric and received wisdom As well as exporting and enforcing a raft of prohibitive policies to all corners of the world, the war on drugs has also exported its own vocabulary. Terms like 'drug', 'addiction' and 'substance abuse' now proliferate in all regions of the world, including Africa, and are anything but straightforward. The word 'drug', for example, is so loaded that anything so labelled (unless it is referring purely to a medicine) is instantly infused with a sinister air. Decades of moral panic about the 'drug menace' – so comically evidenced in such early anti-drug films as *Reefer Madness* – has inculcated the notion that anything labelled a 'drug' is bad. This has led to the conflation of all sorts of substances so labelled – from cannabis to heroin, all 'drugs' are evil, no matter what their individual properties or harm potential. While such substances are conflated, other psychoactive substances – tobacco and alcohol – are categorized separately, and not included in international drug treaties, so betraying the bias of those who drew up the conventions. Another term of 'abuse' is 'narcotic', a word that in a strict sense refers to drugs that induce sleep such as those derived from opium, but has instead become a general term for all restricted drugs, including stimulants such as cocaine and amphetamine. Notions such as 'addiction' are also loaded, promoting the idea that to take a drug is to relinquish control of one's free will.

The drug war rhetoric has not spared the supply side either, describing every person trading or selling drugs as a major 'drug baron', naturally resorting to violence as a means to get ahead in the grand battle between 'cartels' and 'mafias'. This rhetoric has become particularly prevalent in media reporting about West Africa's role in the transit of drugs such as cocaine, and in later chapters we will demonstrate how inaccurate such portrayals are. Little of this stereotyping language reflects the realities of the people using, producing and smuggling drugs, and, in fact, few of these depictions are based on any evidence about drugs and their impact on societies. Such language, however, is often more potent than the substances themselves, and when mobilized in discourse, it has the power to cajole and coerce those who otherwise might be tempted to commit a modern-day sin: being 'soft on drugs'.

As Robin Room shows, national and international debates about drugs at the policy level come with a particular way of thinking and talking about drugs that allows for little deviation from received wisdom.[9] Such discourse is full of Nixon-like phrases of drugs as 'scourges' and 'menaces' that must be battled against in a 'war'. To veer away from a prohibitionist policy is labelled 'surrender'. Of course, such discourse resonates with that of the 'war on terrorism', and the two wars have melded in the form of 'narcoterrorism', a term often applied to the financing of operations of groups such as Colombia's FARC (Fuerzas Armadas Revolucionarias de Colombia) through cocaine smuggling, and fears that al-Qaeda and their ilk are also financed through drugs.

After the terrorist attacks of September 11, a further 'securitization' of western policy towards developing countries has also engulfed drug control. Rhetoric has now shifted away from drugs as a health concern towards a focus on the instability that drug trafficking brings to states, such as Guinea-Bissau, and their fragile economies and how these 'weak states' in Africa offer drug criminals and terrorists 'ungoverned spaces' to act with impunity and threaten the West. Only a war on these criminals, a strengthening of unprepared states in the South and a general tightening of global drug prohibition is said to prevent the unavoidable disaster.

While the genuine dangers of drug use – and the many problem users around the globe – clearly play a role in generating and reinforcing the climate of fear about their use, such loaded discourse and conceptualizations have become hegemonic, allowing little room in corridors of power for alternative approaches to tackling drugs beyond the prohibitive. However, alternative approaches are promoted more and more insistently in expert circles – although not yet in Africa as this book will show – and many have started to perceive the war on drugs as a spectacular failure. Dreams of drug-free societies have dissipated in the face of continued massive production, trafficking and consumption, whereas the nightmare reality of violence in Mexico and elsewhere sustained by aggressive supply-side measures convinces many that there must be a better way.

7

Countercurrents While the debate about policy alternatives has almost been non-existent across Africa, in the countries that have historically driven global drug control, there has always been resistance to the prohibitive measures and rhetoric of the war on drugs. Received wisdom concerning the dangers of drugs has been countered by more positive assessments of the role of drugs in society (especially in regard to drugs such as cannabis and ecstasy), as well as by criticisms of perceived hypocrisy in prohibiting certain drugs, while treating alcohol and tobacco differently. A libertarian position voiced in the US drug policy debate has proposed drug legalization as an alternative to the internationally dominant control approach. These positions have been promoted by some prominent public figures, such as the Nobel Prize-winning economist Milton Friedman. Their proponents argue that the re-legalization of the drug trade would eliminate the existence of criminal markets, which had been a direct consequence of drug prohibition.

Although no country has gone so far as full legalization, there have been some changes in this direction on the national level, in particular towards the so-called 'decriminalization' of drug control. This decriminalization has meant that the criminal justice apparatus – the police, courts and prisons – have gradually handed over their drug control responsibilities to the health sector. While cannabis, cocaine and heroin use, trade and cultivation have remained illegal, users, traders and cultivators, particularly of small amounts of drugs, are not being pursued by the state. Portugal has experimented with the decriminalization of possession with some positive results, as increased emphasis on treatment has apparently led to drops in heroin use and a reduction in the number of drugs deaths;[10] a number of states in the US, and countries around the world, have experimented with legalizing the use of 'medical marijuana'.

Also, especially in the wake of fears concerning the spread of HIV/AIDS through needle-sharing, the concept of 'harm reduction' has gained prominence, whereby rather than campaigning for a 'drug-free' society and 'total abstinence' of users, the emphasis is put on minimizing the harm users might inflict upon themselves and others. Among the many theories and practices of harm reduction, needle exchange programmes for injecting drug users, heroin prescription and methadone maintenance programmes have been the measures most commonly advocated.[11] Harm reduction is practised in several European countries and even in China today and has had some impact on the sidelines of international conferences and on the work of the UNODC, although it rarely made it into official UN policy statements in large parts due to US opposition. While the Bush government resisted calls for harm reduction on the grounds that it tolerates drug use, the Obama administration appears more amenable to such an approach; this policy change in the US, as we shall see in Chapter 1, has ramifications for Africa.[12]

In the last three years, the UNODC's insistence on opposing harm reduction has clearly isolated the organization within the UN system, as most other UN bodies with an interest in the issue, including UNAIDS, WHO and the UN High Commission for Human Rights, have started to criticize the UNODC for its 'ideological opposition' to needle exchange and methadone programmes. This has led to an accentuation of the UNODC's prohibitionist stance and a further polarization of the UN debate about drug policy.[13] One of the consequences of the UNODC's hard line is that substantial funds are still available for African police forces – many of them perceived as corrupt and repressive – but little for medical initiatives to tackle the health-related problems of drug use.

In any case, today there are more diverse views expressed about international drug control than 25 years ago largely because of the growing opposition to the prohibitionist approach.[14] Alternatives to the existing approach started to gain traction in the 1990s with policies that elevated the prevention and reduction of illicit demand as well as drug treatment and rehabilitation to the same level of importance as supply control and the suppression of illicit trafficking. The goal of these policies has been to promote a balance between these aspects of drug control on the

9

international level as well as a more equal relationship between rich and poor states and their respective financial responsibilities for the world drug problem. Clearly this proposed policy change is in the interest of developing states that had been campaigning against the overemphasis on drug supply and the underemphasis on western demand for the substances.[15]

The UN General Assembly Special Session on Drugs in 1998 saw greater emphasis on a more 'balanced' approach. Several of this meeting's declarations proclaimed the importance of demand control, drug use prevention as well as alternative development policies helping to substitute illegal crops with legal ones in the developing world. Many of these statements spoke up for developing and reformist countries in the international system, but in the end the prohibitionist agenda largely won the day, gaining the support of a majority of representatives including many from Africa. The UNODC, seen as a driver of reform at the time, succumbed to the pressures from the US government and excelled itself in coining the conference slogan: 'a drug-free world, we can do it'.[16] However, in the wake of significant anniversaries in the history of drug control – the 100th anniversary of the 1912 Hague treaty, and the 50th anniversary of the 1961 convention – many commentators have appraised the war on drugs and labelled it a failure. Rather than governments, it has been NGOs who have been at the forefront of demands for an international rethink in policy. These include the International Drug Policy Consortium that promotes open debate on drug policy, and Count the Costs, an organization formed to mark the 50th anniversary of the 1961 convention that campaigned for an end to the drug war.[17]

Despite the efforts of such organizations, from a purely legal perspective these policy debates as well as related international demand control statements in the 1990s have so far had only limited effects on the global drug control regime and its supply control bias. They have not introduced any new binding mechanisms and institutions. This is even more striking when strong pressures from some developing countries – though not from African governments – for the drafting of a demand reduction treaty to balance the 1988 convention are considered. Such pressures were not strong enough and could not seriously challenge US, European and their allies' opposition to drastic policy change.[18] Hence, the international promotion of drug demand reduction did not reach the same status as supply control in 1998, and the standard policy approach of the war on drugs remains mainstream. This is despite the growing international movement questioning the effectiveness of the war on drugs.[19] The drug war may be widely seen as a failure, but an admission of surrender is not imminent.

Africa and the drugs war

Despite high-profile global campaigns about the inefficacy of the war on drugs, the war on drugs has only intensified in Africa in the wake of concern about the continent as *entrepôt*, concern crystallized in the increasing focus on Africa in the UNODC's *World Drug Report*, and in such publications as *The Drugs Nexus in Africa* and *Cannabis in Africa* since the late 1990s. Such publications on drugs on the continent, as well as so-called national 'rapid situation assessments', still constitute the bulk of accessible literature available on drugs in Africa, although even their authors have lamented the inadequacy of such research exercises: '[T]he short timeframe, the number of countries covered and the number of actors involved in fact-finding and analysis limited the output of this exercise to a brief snapshot'.[20]

The following chapters will deal in detail with the limitations of these 'snapshots' of African drugs, as we argue that many of these reports are based on outdated – since the late 1990s little new empirical research has been conducted by the UN – and unreliable data. Drug use data and information about the cultivation of drugs on the continent have largely been ignored due to a lack of donor and African government interest. Since the mid-2000s a few UN studies have dealt with the most worrying aspect of drugs for the international donor community: the transit trade in heroin and cocaine; however, even here these reports have too heavily relied on seizure and arrest data that are highly problematic sources of information. Official research has commonly ignored the viewpoints of the users, traders and cultivators of drugs themselves as well as the long history of drugs on the continent. This book aims to fill some of these gaps in our understanding.

The existing academic literature on this topic is even more limited, although there has been a recent effort to place drugs on the continent into the broader historical and cultural context. Most extensive is the literature on legal drugs, such as alcohol, kola and khat, with social historians of alcohol in particular contributing to our understanding of the complexities of the use, trade, production and control of the continent's favourite legal substance.[21] Work on the light stimulants khat and kola has similarly benefited from easier access to sources and a contemporary interest in these drugs with a long history on the continent. In contrast, the research effort on cannabis, cocaine and heroin can only be seen as an 'emerging field'. In South Africa, cannabis has been studied by a few anthropologists, while historians have highlighted the extensive roots of heroin, cocaine as well as cannabis in West Africa.[22] Some of this academic research, in particular the recent work on the heroin and cocaine transit trade, has to some degree been driven by policy concerns of international organizations and national governments, which is most clearly symbolized by its heavy reliance on problematic government data on drugs. In any case, far too little research has until now been conducted to allow for an 'evidence-based drug policy' in African countries. Instead, there has been a heavy reliance on experiences and models from other regions, as this book will argue.

However, what evidence there is suggests that actual drug policy in Africa – although varied and often subverted or neglected in practice – remains principally focused on repressive supply-side interventions, and harsh prison terms are usually mandated even for minor possession of cannabis. Although there is a decriminalization movement in South Africa,[23] alternative voices are rarely heard in the rest of the continent, and harm reduction initiatives such as needle exchange are conspicuous by their absence, despite the high rates of blood-borne diseases among injecting drug users. There is call from drug practitioners for more resources to be spent on drug treatment and educational campaigns, but limited resources mean that the recent methadone treatment programme in Dar es Salaam is unlikely to be implemented elsewhere in the near future. With few dedicated treatment facilities, many problem users find themselves admitted to psychiatric hospitals or left by themselves. Furthermore, as mentioned above, the perception is promoted within the continent and beyond that Africa is on the verge of a crisis of drugs and crime, as production, smuggling and use of psychoactive substances is reckoned on the rise with a consequent impact on the prospects of development, although again, little of this crisis talk is based on evidence or serious research about drugs in Africa.

As this book will show, the story of the African war on drugs is not a uniform or just a recent one: it has played out in different ways in different countries, and in some cases it has a long history. Prohibitive policies against certain drugs go back almost a century, as colonial powers adopted prohibitive policies towards them in the first half of the twentieth century. Also, the prohibitionist push of the war on drugs has not been forced on all psychoactive substances viewed with suspicion: the case of the stimulant khat in East Africa – regarded as a 'drug of abuse' by many – and the resistance of its farmers, traders and consumers to its absorption into the range of drugs to be fought is a case in point that we shall focus on later in this book. Turning a blind eye to the production of cannabis where it is a region's major cash crop shows that the war on drugs is sometimes fought only in rhetoric. Also, international treaties give some flexibility to governments in how they are actualized: there are a variety of drug control practices across Africa, as instanced by the repressive Nigerian and a more medically oriented Tanzanian drug policy. Our book analyses the drug situation in Africa, exploring the ambiguities hidden underneath the supposed certainties of the drugs war; it will examine the extent of policies followed and their alternatives, and asks the following key questions:

13

- What is the historical depth to African drug production, trade, consumption and policy?
- What is the extent of drug consumption in Africa? What substances are consumed in what socio-cultural settings? And how fearful should we be?
- How damaging to development are the production, trade and use of drugs in Africa?
- Will Africa's role as *entrepôt* in the trade of heroin and cocaine further expand and lead to the emergence of 'narco-states'?
- How has the war on drugs manifested itself in different African countries? And how have different states actualized international drug policy?
- What room is there in Africa for alternative perspectives and policies that diverge from the received wisdom of prohibition?

In answering these questions, the book divides its focus into the use of drugs in Africa, drug cultivation, the trade through the continent, and state responses to drugs. Chapter 1 introduces the reader to the types of drugs used, and shows that the moral panic about the potential of such consumption to tear African societies apart is exaggerated, although problem consumers – whether of licit alcohol or illicit heroin – have few treatment options as current policy is so weighted towards supply-side intervention. Chapter 2 questions the evidence base of the received wisdom of drugs as harmful to development in Africa, as it discusses how drug production – while viewed with a jaundiced eye in the wider world – offers support to many in the wake of economic hardship. Chapter 3 explores the continent's role as a transit point in drugs and, by introducing actual traders of heroin and cocaine, it challenges problematic depictions of African 'drug barons' and 'cartels' widespread in the drug war vocabulary, as well as the common assumption that Africa's role in the global trade in drugs is destined to increase in future years. Chapter 4 assesses the efforts of African states in the drugs war, which range from neglect of the trade, through complicity, to the enactment of oppressively harsh punitive measures. In the last case, drug policy can be more harmful than the drugs themselves. Meanwhile, possible alternative policies are almost entirely ignored in the African context as the drugs war rhetoric has stifled debate in Africa about drugs and how they are dealt with.

1 | Africa's drug habit

[T]here is now the risk of a public health disaster in developing countries that would enslave masses of humanity to the misery of drug dependence. (Antonio Maria Costa, Executive Director, UNODC)[1]

Teens Frenzied in Drug Abuse (Website of National Campaign Against Drug Abuse Authority, Kenya)[2]

In the last decade, Africa's association with drugs has revolved primarily around the continent's role as a transit hub in the global trade of cocaine and heroin; in contrast, consumption within the continent has been low down the list of global priorities. Consequently, Africa's relationship with drugs often seems a function of demand in western countries. In this chapter, we bring Africa's own 'drug habit' to the foreground, following our general approach of examining the drug situation in Africa from an Africa-centric perspective. Drug use is certainly an issue of great concern within Africa, as demonstrated by the torrent of media reports by local outlets. Most of these reports are infused with the discourse of the war on drugs, and moral panic is evident in such reporting: drug abuse is destroying Africa's youth, making them 'frenzied' in the above words of Kenya's anti-drug agency, National Campaign Against Drug Abuse Authority. Africa is presented as threatened as never before by a crisis of drink and drugs.[3]

This stereotypical portrayal of substance use in Africa does little justice to the complexity of the topic, conflating the myriad substances consumed in a diverse set of contexts into a western-derived model of addiction and pharmacological determinism. This chapter challenges this model, introducing the reader to a number of substances and their cultures of consumption, showing

16

how intertwined certain substances are with African cultures and societies, and the historical depth of Africa's relationship with drugs: the use of certain substances goes back at least centuries. While recently introduced substances such as heroin and methamphetamine are justifiably of great concern, their conflation with other substances with more established histories in Africa – khat and cannabis, for example – leads to very skewed perspectives on these 'softer' drugs. After a section examining the interactions of chemicals, culture and society in drug use, we provide a survey of several important substances consumed in Africa. First, however, we look at the type of sources available for the history and contemporary patterns and trends of African substance use.

Sources for African drug consumption

In surveying Africa's historical and contemporary drug use, we make use of a wide variety of sources. The extent and reliability of source material is patchy, although for some substances it is more comprehensive than for others: for example, we know much more about alcohol and khat use compared with cannabis, despite the ubiquity of the last of these. Clearly this reflects difficulties in studying an illicit substance, as well as the priorities of funding bodies and researchers. For all substances, however, source material for pre-modern usage is the most scanty, although we know from archaeological research in other parts of the world that humanity's relationship with psychoactive substances stretches back millennia.[4] Indeed, an ancient beginning for our drug and alcohol habit is certain: by the Neolithic period, 'cannabis, opium, betel, tobacco and even fermented alcoholic drinks were widely used'.[5]

Regarding Sub-Saharan Africa, archaeological evidence is very limited, the best being a number of pipe bowls found with traces of cannabis dating from around 1400 in central Ethiopia.[6] We have to rely instead on oral historical accounts of early substance use (for example, accounts of khat use in pre-colonial Kenya), and the writings of early visitors to the continent. Perhaps the earliest such source is the twelfth-century account of a Spanish doctor – El-Ghafeky – who refers to kola, while the Moroccan explorer, Ibn Battuta, reports being offered what appears to be betel nut to chew in Mogadishu in the fourteenth century, and an Ethiopian chronicle of the same century refers to the stimulant khat.[7] Later European writings give further tantalizing glimpses of psychoactive substance use. For example, seventeenth-century reports from southern Africa refer to the root of a shrub called *canna* – a psychoactive member of the *Mesembryanthemum* genus – chewed by Khoikhoi. Some speculate that *canna* was an important commodity traded among groups in southern Africa in pre-colonial times.[8] Reports of tobacco and cannabis use are also present in the exploration literature, cannabis being widely diffused in southern and eastern Africa, while tobacco cultivation and use had spread continent-wide through sixteenth- and seventeenth-century contact with the Portuguese.[9] There are references to other plants used in southern Africa at this time, including species of *datura*, a member of the nightshade family familiar for its long, white trumpet-shaped flowers, whose dangerous alkaloids can generate powerful hallucinations. The use of khat in Kenya is also referred to by explorers in the late nineteenth century who reached the Nyambene Hills where it is still cultivated and consumed by the Meru people of central Kenya. While such sparse evidence can only hint at the full extent of drug use in pre-colonial Africa, and identifying plants from accounts of travellers is fraught with problems, we can extrapolate from these glimpses and the extensive contemporary pharmacopeia of many African societies, that knowledge of such substances was widespread, and that many were incorporated into the fabric of social and economic life.

Regarding the contemporary situation, despite growing alarm at an 'epidemic' of drug use in Africa, information upon which to assess trends in consumption is patchy and hard to generalize from. Of course, estimating demand and consumption trends of usually illicitly supplied commodities is hugely difficult, and the UNODC has moved in the last three years from giving point estimates regarding drug prevalence, to instead giving large estimate ranges: they themselves are clearly aware of the difficulties in providing accurate statistics regarding drugs. Much of the statistical information used to observe trends in global demand and supply is provided each year in the UNODC's World Drug Report (WDR). The neutrality of the WDR is doubtful, and pressure placed on those drafting it to adhere to the current status quo in international policy has been recounted by one of those previously involved in writing it (who subsequently resigned).[10] Aside from doubts about its neutrality, the statistics used in WDRs are themselves open to criticism. These are based on responses by individual governments to questionnaires, the Annual Report Questionnaires. The methodology sections of the last few WDRs provide maps showing which countries have filled in the questionnaires either fully or partly, and African countries with thoroughgoing responses are well in the minority. In the WDR of 2010, only 30 per cent of African countries submitted their reports compared with much higher percentages for Europe, North America and Asia. Also, in the words of the International Drug Policy Consortium (IDPC), a grouping of drug NGOs, in their response to the 2010 WDR, 'the quality of information provided on illicit drug supply is significantly better than data provided on drug use related information ... this is one of the consequences of the historical dominance of a drug control policy directed at the suppression of supply'.[11]

To make up for this data deficit, further research and initiatives like South Africa's South African Community Epidemiology Network on Drug Use (SACENDU)[12] that surveys and publishes reports on trends in drug use make a real difference. Despite the glaring holes in statistical data, other sources – academic dissertations, articles and books, media reports, grey literature, online sources and so forth – do provide much useful information and help form the foundation for this chapter.

Understanding drug use

The word 'drug' comes with plenty of baggage. It can conjure up the stereotypical portrayal of the addict compelled to seek out his or her next fix of the controlling chemical, and suggests the simplistic notion that those unfortunate enough to try a 'drug' become hooked and compelled to continue its use. This image is as potent in Africa as elsewhere, promoted in the media, and in anti-drugs campaigns. The war on drugs has led to a discourse where substance use is often reduced to pharmacology and this medicalized notion of addiction. In such a discourse, the explanation for drug use is all in the chemistry.

Of course, the psychoactive and physiological effects of drugs cannot be ignored, and a grasp of their pharmacological action is essential in understanding their appeal and dangers for African consumers. The ability of natural and synthetic compounds such as cocaine and methamphetamine to mimic brain chemicals, in particular those related to the release of dopamine and other compounds related to the 'reward centre' of the brain, powerfully explains the 'rush' and 'high' so often described by consumers. The similarity of opiate drugs to the brain's natural painkillers – endorphins – also explains how they can induce feelings of euphoria and dampen out both physical and psychological pain.[13] The actions of such isolated chemicals are easier to understand than the combination of active compounds in such plant substances as cannabis, khat and even tea, where the effects of certain compounds appear to counteract those of others, and scientific experiments that take these different factors into account are difficult to devise. However, even here much progress has been made, and, for example, we now have a better grasp of how other compounds present in cannabis can moderate effects of its most studied compound: tetrahydrocannabinol. While the effects of such substances vary greatly depending on the individual consumer (due to idiosyncrasies in body weight, metabolism, as well as set and setting[14]), there is still sufficient convergence in their actions for pharmacology to offer much essential insight in studying the whys and wherefores of their consumption, whether this consumption takes place in London or Lagos.

But psychoactive substances are soaked in sociality and culture, and understanding fully the effects and appeal of their pharmacology requires understanding the social and cultural contexts in which the drugs are consumed, many of which aren't recreational, but instead ritualistic or functional. As we will see below, cannabis consumption in Africa is often used to increase stamina, rather than in the recreational settings associated with the drug in the West. Also, attempts to explain too much through pharmacology can lead to reductionist theories that don't do justice to the sheer variety of factors influencing consumption and how problematic or otherwise it becomes. For example, theorizing that alcohol leads to disinhibition in its consumers has been critiqued extensively by anthropologists and others who point out the cultural variation in intoxicated behaviour and ideas about intoxication.[15] The anthropological commonplace that people perceive and feel the effects of drugs – whether medicinal or recreational – through cultural filters is hardly a radical theory, but it is still a powerful counter to a pharmacological deterministic approach to drug use. The potential complexity that culture brings to perceptions of drugs is nicely demonstrated by the famous 'placebo effect' in medicine, and how meanings associated with, for example, the colour and taste of medicines can increase or impede their efficacy is well attested.[16] The pharmacologies of drugs certainly help constitute the ideas and cultural worlds built around them; but ideas, meanings and associations in turn help constitute how these pharmacologies are felt and described. Even perceiving pleasure from the effects of drug use is not a simple matter, as Howard Becker demonstrated in his famous article of how people had to learn to become cannabis smokers – they had to learn how to inhale smoke, and to be socialized into feeling certain effects that might not be inherently pleasurable (dizziness, for example) as something to enjoy.[17]

While anthropologists have been keen in general to relativize drug consumption, other approaches in the social sciences have been keen to have their say in explaining drug use. The importance of concepts such as 'social exclusion' and 'anomie' in such theories shows how the notion of drug use as something 'deviant' has a hold on people's perceptions, despite the near ubiquity of drug use in human society. Such approaches also downplay one of the main reasons for using such substances – pleasure; indeed, hedonism swirls around drug cultures such as that of Kenya, where consumers of alcohol, cannabis, heroin and khat all strive to induce the euphoric feeling of *stimu* (from the English word 'steam'), the general term used for intoxication. However, understanding the social settings of drug consumption is crucial, as is understanding the impacts of consumption for sociality and issues of poverty, well-being and power. Substance use clearly has much potential for social harm – especially where the substance itself comes to dominate a life – while it can also have a positive side, helping forge social networks, ward off fatigue and so forth. Social exclusion can be an important factor in drug use, but so can social inclusion, and problematic drug use is certainly not restricted to those deemed as 'socially excluded' or suffering from 'anomie'. There is no social theory of drug use that can account for all the particularities of each substance in each particular social and cultural setting. For example, the social and cultural worlds revolving around khat and cannabis in Africa (see below) often diverge from western ideas of what drug consumption involves, and one can't just assume that concepts such as 'addiction', 'anomie' or 'social exclusion' will explain satisfactorily their continuing popularity.

Nevertheless, there is convergence in African and western drug cultures. This convergence is seen in the similar modes of con-sumption used for particular drugs (smoking and injecting), and in similarities in the way particular drug effects are described. Descriptions of the (pharmacological and social) effects of heroin appear very similar in Africa as elsewhere, for example, as do those of methamphetamine in South Africa. Such convergence comes both from the effects of the substances, and from the globalization of drugs discourse. Another globalized feature of Africa's drug cultures is the embrace of reggae culture and its extolling of cannabis use. Also, poverty and social exclusion do play important roles – though not necessarily causal ones – in problematic consumption in Africa, as they do in the West; where much meaning and respect revolves around gangs, and where drugs are as easily accessible as in such deprived and marginalized areas as South Africa's Cape Flats, high rates of drug use are to be expected. And poverty is a considerable barrier to treatment for drug problems; as such treatment is generally only available for those few who can afford it.

In short, understanding demand for psychoactive substances in Africa requires a grasp of pharmacological, cultural, social and political-economic factors, and the way these interact. Sadly, the available research is not yet of sufficient depth in respect to many of these substances, but what follows will provide the reader with an overview of drug use in Africa: the many different types of intoxicating and stimulating substances used, their histories and social importance and the many different cultures of consumption that revolve around them.

Key substances

In this section, we focus in detail on some of the key substances used in Sub-Saharan Africa – khat, cannabis, heroin, cocaine, mandrax and methamphetamine – that are most targeted by the war on drugs. However, these are not the only 'drugs' used in Africa, and numerous other psychoactive substances are widely consumed. In what follows we also introduce the reader to some of these other substances too, beginning with those containing caffeine, which while of little danger to the health of consumers, are of great social significance. We also focus on two other legal, but more ambivalently regarded, substances: alcohol and tobacco. These are usually insulated from comparison with illicit psychoactive substances, but concerns about their health and social impact are leading to more and more campaigns for their tighter regulation. We then look at khat, a substance labelled as 'quasi-legal' as its legality varies so much from country to country. The other substances covered are those more widely condemned and under international control. Though, as we will see in the case of cannabis, its long history and its cultural validation among many on the continent means that it is soaked in

23

much ambivalence too. Of course, we miss out many important and fascinating substances in the descriptions below, in particular *iboga* (the roots of *Taberbanthe iboga*, a hallucinogen used in the Bwiti cult of Gabon),[18] solvents used by street children in Africa and throughout the developing world, and such pharmaceuticals as Rohypnol and diazepam, sold illegally and used recreationally in countries including Kenya.

The legal

AFRICA'S CAFFEINE FIX Caffeine is the world's most consumed psychoactive substance, its mildly stimulating properties appreciated globally both for their pragmatic use in various work contexts, and for the sociality and culture embodied in the substances containing the compound and the rituals of their consumption. Africa has as much of a caffeine habit as elsewhere in the world. While coffee drinking is said to have Yemeni origin, the plant itself is reckoned indigenous to Ethiopia, and the coffee bean and ceremonies surrounding it are still very much valued as part of the culture and economy of its people. Coffee drinking almost certainly diffused among Muslims in Ethiopia's eastern highlands over the course of the sixteenth century,[19] while coffee beans have been consumed ritually in such ceremonies as *buna qalla* ('the sacrifice of the coffee beans') among Oromo.[20] Beyond Ethiopia, coffee is a common cash crop, but not commonly drunk except in the guise of instant coffee, although South Africa, Kenya and elsewhere have western-style coffee shops popular with the middle classes. Tea is far more widely drunk having spread throughout the continent, and is consumed in a variety of fashions, from the milky sweet *chai* of East Africa to the minty *attaya* of Senegal.

West and central Africa has its own caffeinated substance in the form of kola. Unlike tea and coffee, these nuts (most commonly harvested from two varieties of trees, *cola nitida* and *cola acuminata*) are consumed by chewing and are not infused into a beverage. Its use is of great antiquity, and 'has been consumed in the western Sudan for at least a millennium and in the central Sudan ... for at least 500 years'.[21] Its bitter taste did not put off consumers, drawn to it for its stimulating constituents and its ability to function as a social stimulant in Islamic regions where alcohol use was forbidden. It became a trade commodity covering vast distances, and wrapped up well in damp packaging, the nuts could survive long journeys through desert from its production zones in modern-day Sierra Leone, Liberia and Ghana, and it even reached as far as North Africa where it entered into the Islamic *materia medica*.[22] In central Sudan, it was at first a luxury good, only used by the elite who could afford it, although this changed in the twentieth century, when it became an item of mass consumption. Its fame spread in the nineteenth century, thanks in great part to its inclusion in the original recipe for Coca Cola. Its production also spread to South America and Madagascar, where it can still be bought today at numerous markets. While its consumption never caught on in the West – although it is consumed by members of the West African diaspora – its social and cultural importance has not dimmed in Africa, and it continues its role in ceremonies (in particular marriage ceremonies), maintaining great symbolic prestige, and being a crucial element of gift exchange. As a caffeinated substance, it has also proved popular among labourers and others for its stamina-boosting properties, and has even been used by warriors to enhance their fighting capabilities.

ALCOHOL AND TOBACCO The popularity of stimulants such as kola and khat (see below) in Muslim areas of Africa has been explained by arguing that they are substitutes for the forbidden alcohol. While such an argument can be overegged – and ignores the many non-Muslims who use these stimulants too – it is certainly true that in non-Islamic areas of Africa, alcohol is the social stimulant *par excellence*. It almost certainly has a very ancient history, and some suggest that brewing beer might have begun at around the same time as the spread of agriculture. Millet, sorghum, maize, honey and bananas have all been used to brew beer, while palm wine is tapped along much of Africa's coastline, East and West. Distillation is a far more recent innovation, but one that has been embraced, with many homemade stills producing strong, cheap and often notorious liquors.

While traditionally brewed beers have remained popular in Africa (usually being much cheaper than manufactured bottled beer) despite many measures against 'local brews' that blur the definition of alcohol as 'licit', western-style bottled beers and spirits have become exceedingly popular too. In countries such as Kenya, consumption of such drinks was restricted to Europeans by law in colonial times, but then was encouraged with advertising campaigns linking brands of beer such as Kenya's Tusker and Nigeria's Star with building a strong postcolonial nation. The legality of 'local brews' and spirits remains contentious in some countries, and in Kenya it is suggested that the infamous liquor *chang'aa* (home-distilled spirit made from grain, and sometimes adulterated with industrial alcohol, sold cheaply, occasionally to deadly effect) should be legalized and regulated to ensure it is a pure product.

A common refrain in African discourse concerning alcohol is that consumption was more socially integrated in earlier times, while modernity has led to increased immoderate and socially damaging consumption. Such a claim often consists of statements that 'beer used to belong to elders', and that the spread of youthful consumption is a symbol and cause of moral decay. As Justin Willis makes clear, such notions of pre-colonial temperance probably do not tally with actual practices in earlier times, where immoderate consumption, and use by youth, almost certainly also occurred.[23] Worries about immoderate consumption are likely as old as alcohol consumption itself.

Alcohol's social and cultural importance in Africa has generated many important studies. In southern Africa a key focus has been on the link between alcoholic drinks and the control of labour, a link most obviously seen in the notorious 'dop system' where farm workers on vineyards would be paid for their services with low-grade wine.[24] This system – now illegal – is reckoned the source of much alcohol dependence among such farm workers.[25] In West Africa, Emmanuel Akyeampong's historical study of alcohol in Ghana provides a rich analysis of its societal importance over the course of two centuries.[26] As in Willis's analysis of East Africa, alcohol consumption in Ghana was also a source of social struggle between elders and younger generations, while its later history is intertwined with resistance to colonial restrictions on African consumption, and attempts by women to access alcoholic drinks, subverting gender relations in the process. Thus, alcohol consumption links in myriad ways to issues of power, as dominant groups, African and European, attempted to control its consumption in Ghana. Resistance to imposed restrictions on consumption has also been analysed in the southern African context, where:

> [i]llegal drinking places became sites for what James Scott describes as the 'hidden transcript' of the dominated: a discourse of opposition that encompassed not only the web of alcohol legislation, but the shared experience of racial oppression and economic exploitation that bound drinkers together.[27]

Of course, not all consumption is quite so political, as Lynn Schler emphasizes in an analysis of consumption in Douala in colonial Cameroon. In the context of a district occupied by immigrants from throughout West Africa, drinking was not so much a site of resistance, but rather 'an important expression of community life that was present-based and practical'.[28]

Whether an expression of community life or of resistance, the ubiquity of alcoholic beverages in many African countries, the many cultures of consumption surrounding them, and the huge economic importance of their licit and illicit production and trade, mean that such drinks and their social significance continue to attract historians and social anthropologists to their study.[29] While such authors tend to play down the notion that Africa has a 'drinking crisis', most would agree that there are significant gaps in our knowledge of African drinking practices, and that there undoubtedly is much risky consumption. Thus, while alcohol is by far the most studied of all African stimulants and intoxicants, much work still needs to be done, especially from a public health perspective.

27

Tobacco consumption in Africa has been little researched in comparison with alcohol, but it has a long history in the continent and its use and continued promotion by tobacco firms is becoming more controversial and subject to restriction. There are many histories yet to be told of tobacco's spread in the continent, although a leaflet from the Field Museum of Natural History published in 1930 pulls together much material on African tobacco use from the early seventeenth century onwards, and makes clear how quickly tobacco was taken up throughout Africa once introduced from South America by the Portuguese and others.[30] Today, trade networks bring chewing tobacco and snuff to even the remotest areas of the continent, while cigarettes are ubiquitous despite growing attempts to curb smoking, most notably in Kenya and South Africa, where its use in public spaces in urban areas is regulated. In Kenya, this is both a public health measure and an effort to beautify the nation by ridding it of discarded cigarette butts. Some tobacco products have been subject to bans too, including *gutka* – Indian-made sachets containing tobacco, areca nut and flavourings – a substance still sold openly in Kenya despite an apparent ban.

The quasi-legal

KHAT Khat is the most commonly used name for the stimulant stems and leaves of the shrub *Catha edulis* which is found growing wild from the Middle East down to the Eastern Cape, and is now cultivated intensively in Yemen, Ethiopia, Kenya, Uganda and northern Madagascar. It seems that cultivation of the substance began in Ethiopia from where the earliest written records of it emerge (from the fourteenth century), though it appears to have quickly spread to Yemen. In Kenya (where it is known as *miraa*) it was already being cultivated and consumed by the Meru in the Nyambene Hills north-east of Mount Kenya when European explorers first reached there in the late nineteenth century, and most likely cultivation began there well before that date. The fresh product is masticated and formed into a plug from which its active compounds seep into the bloodstream. Its most potent compound, *cathinone*, acts like a mild amphetamine, increasing levels of dopamine in the brain and so leading to increased wakefulness, as well as a general sense of euphoria. Its effects are described as *mirqaan* or *markana* in Somalia and Ethiopia, and *handas* in Kenya.

Perceptions of this stimulant are polarized: some see it as a noxious drug destroying health and the social fabric, while others extol its virtues as a mild stimulant whose consumption binds people together. The former point to khat's association with a wealth of health problems and social harms. Health problems range from dental pathologies (khat is often chewed with sugar, bubblegum or sweet drinks to mask its astringent taste), to insomnia and even psychosis. Consumers often have ways to counteract insomnia by ceasing chewing well before bedtime, or consuming beer to knock off the 'high'. Research into more serious problems such as the link with psychotic episodes is cautious in ascribing a causal link, although it may be a contributory factor alongside underlying mental health problems and exposure to traumatic situations.[31] Regarding social harms, it is linked with family breakups, as chewers – the majority of whom are male, although there are many women chewers – are said to spend long times away from the home, and unemployment, as khat is associated with idleness. Income diversion is also seen as a major problem in countries such as Djibouti, where a large proportion of household income (around a third in some estimates) is spent on khat.[32]

While there certainly are 'problem users' who chew at the expense of food (khat – like other stimulants – reduces appetite) and sleep, making it hard for them to hold down work, assessing the extent of associated 'social harms' is difficult as evidence in Africa and among diaspora populations of khat consumers is often mixed and contradictory.[33] More positively, some point to its link to cultural identity and its role in bringing people together in peaceful gatherings where amity is generated and advice proffered. Going even further, some have described khat as playing a positive role in uniting people in Somaliland and helping that breakaway country's path to peace.[34] This contrasts strongly with khat's presentation to the outside world as a drug associated with war in Somalia, where some reporting led to its being portrayed as a root cause of the conflict in the early 1990s. This link with war and peace demonstrates well the general ambivalence with which debate about khat is infused.

Concern about associated problems, and the conflation of khat with other substances, has led to a number of attempts to prohibit the substance in East Africa and the Horn of Africa.[35] Many of these attempts failed – most notably in colonial Kenya and Somaliland – although khat remains illegal in a number of African countries, including Tanzania and Eritrea. There are no internationally valid laws against khat itself, although the addition of khat's two main chemicals to international schedules of restricted substances led a number of countries in North America and Europe to ban the plant itself. The growth of diaspora communities in Western countries – especially in the wake of the collapse of Somalia in the early 1990s – has led to demand for the substance in such countries, and this continues despite its illegality in many of them. It still remains legal in the UK where there is a very large Somali diaspora community. Khat's varied legal status has led to its being termed a 'quasi-legal' substance: one whose legal status varies greatly between jurisdictions and over time.[36]

Khat's pharmacology has allowed it to become incorporated into a wide range of social and cultural contexts, ceremonial, recreational and work-related. It is widely used in functional ways, its stimulating properties appreciated by nightwatchmen, lorry drivers and even revising students. It is likely that its stimulating properties have been utilized by different groups for centuries, especially by hunter-gatherers with great botanical knowledge. Its consumption in Ethiopia was until the second half of the twentieth century mainly associated with Islamic ceremonies, where it helped attendees remain wakeful for prayers, and it also features prominently at spirit possession ceremonies in Ethiopia, Somalia and northern Kenya. Among the Meru of Kenya, khat has great symbolic importance, and special bundles of khat known as *ncoolo* are still presented between parties and chewed at brideprice negotiations and other occasions. Of course, much consumption is recreational: chewing khat in company over a number of hours leads to increased conviviality. The 'khat party', where groups of chewers spend their leisure time chewing together, is an institutionalized feature of life not just in the Yemen (where much of the literature is focused), but also in Djibouti, Ethiopia, Somalia, Somaliland, Kenya, Uganda and Madagascar. Such parties often last for the whole evening or afternoon (so leading to the concern with reduced productivity of the workforce), and can take place in homes (women chewers often prefer to chew in private at home as their consumption is often frowned upon) or in public places. For example, in Lamu in Kenya, much consumption can be seen of an evening along the harbour road, as men gather to chew and converse, perhaps slaking their thirst at the same time with sweet coffee or soda. Such parties range from rather formal occasions where people are seated in a circle, sometimes in hierarchical order, while supplies of khat are laid out in front of them. Many sessions are much more informal, however, with chewers sitting in cafes, perhaps watching football or the news on television.

As mentioned above, khat consumption is often seen as principally a Muslim habit, it taking the place of the forbidden alcohol as a social stimulant. However, while it is used extensively by Muslim Somalis, Oromo and East Africans of Arab descent, its use crosses religious, ethnic and social divides. For example, in Kenya its use has spread throughout the country, being popular in the area where it is most intensively cultivated (Meru District), the north inhabited by Muslim pastoralists, the coast with its large Muslim population, and in urban centres where it is very popular as part of a youth culture. In fact, in much of the region, khat is now seen as 'cool' (*poa* in Kiswahili), and khat takes its place alongside other accessories of a globalized youth culture. Some argue that khat's 'traditional' consumption in ceremonial or religious contexts was thoroughly regulated by cultural norms, while youthful consumption was limited as it was restricted to elders. As with alcohol, the discourse of a former socially integrated consumption contrasting with unrestrained and dangerous youthful consumption today is widespread, and relies on a good deal of nostalgic idealizing of the past.

Khat has an interesting link with class in East Africa. Many wealthier Kenyans look down upon the substance as a low-class substance associated with the Muslim north and Somalis, as well as the urban underclass. Interestingly, while khat has spread among workers performing such roles as bus drivers or conductors, and even sex workers, in areas where it is produced or consumed, knowledge of the many different varieties (which range in Kenya from the *matako* or 'buttocks' of khat sold cheaply, to very expensive varieties that can retail for the equivalent of £8–10 and are compared by consumers to fine wine) means that wealthier consumers can indulge in some 'conspicuous consumption', safe in the knowledge that those around them will see the high class of their khat. Thus, khat consumption is not just an activity of the poor, but one of the wealthy too. However, it is still tinged in the eyes of many in East Africa as being not quite 'respectable', and abhorred by some as a 'drug'. Also, churches – especially evangelical or Pentecostal denominations – and conservative Islamic clerics play a large role in campaigning against its consumption. Such a lack of 'respectability' – in the genteel sense – goes some way to explaining the 'respect' – in the 'cool' sense – shown to it in East African youth culture.

The illegal

CANNABIS Cannabis is by far the most widely consumed illicit substance in Africa, as it is elsewhere in the world, and the UNODC estimates that in 2005 there were 38.2 million cannabis users in Africa, 7.7 per cent of the 15–64 aged population.[37] A 1999 report on drugs in Africa that surveyed ten countries (Kenya, South Africa, Zimbabwe, Nigeria, Cameroon, Mozambique, Ethiopia, Ghana, Côte d'Ivoire and Senegal) found cannabis produced and consumed (mainly by smoking) in all ten, and sold very cheaply, usually much cheaper than bottled beer, making it highly accessible.[38] Its popularity with youth is especially high, data from 2004 suggesting that 18.9 per cent of young Kenyans had used it at least once in their lifetime, with similar figures from Madagascar and Ghana.[39] Large quantities are seized – especially in South Africa and Nigeria – but supply remains unaffected, and while those caught in possession are sometimes incarcerated,[40] fear of arrest hardly seems to dent its popularity; cannabis appears deprioritized by law enforcement in a number of African countries, although the recent international concern has meant that cannabis consumers and farmers have been the easiest targets for African drug enforcers and there are many seizures of the drug.[41] Indeed, Table 1.1 is illustrative of cannabis's status as the number one illicit substance in Africa, showing cannabis seizures far outstripping those of other drugs.

In eastern and southern Africa, cannabis has a very long history, as the traces on Ethiopian pottery from the fourteenth century reveal (see above), while in southern Africa research suggests cannabis was used by San and Khoikoi people well before AD 1500;[42] it was no doubt introduced through the Indian Ocean trade networks and Arabs who settled on the eastern African coast, from there percolating southwards and westwards.[43] In Madagascar, its consumption is known from the mid-seventeenth century,[44] while in central Africa, cannabis was integrated into a charismatic movement of the Bashilange known as the *Bene Diamba* ('children of hemp' – *diamba* being a variant of a common term for cannabis in central Africa), whose ceremonies suffused with cannabis smoke were bemusedly recorded by nineteenth-century explorers.[45] Throughout the region, cannabis was not just used for its intoxicating properties, but also as a medicine, and many traditional healers – such as the *sangoma* of southern Africa – still use all parts of the plant to cure various ailments. It was commonly reported in the literature of explorers that cannabis was smoked by warriors before raids, although its use by praise singers and by people requiring deep thought to solve problems was also reported.[46] Despite the imposition of legal restrictions on cannabis production and consumption in Africa over the course of the twentieth century, it is as ubiquitous as ever, and as we

TABLE 1.1 Drug seizures in Africa (kilograms), 2005–09

	2005	2006	2007	2008	2009	% of global total in 2009
Cannabis herb	865,974	1,220,578	694,177	936,084	639,769	11.0
Cannabis resin	121,576	132,784	140,544	165,455	320,600	25.0
Khat	1,522	5,691	2,490	6,219	23,442	12.0
Cocaine	2,575	851	5,535	2,551	956	0.1
Methaqualone	159	773	93	1,586	828	99.0
Heroin	325	335	328	311	515	0.7
Opium	45	33	49	67	57	0.01
Amphetamines	2,085	851	721	3,492	98	0.2
Ecstasy	3.7	74.5	9.2	0.06	0.02	0.0

Source: UNODC, *WDR 2011*

shall see in Chapter 2, offers many farmers a livelihood from western Kenya to Lesotho. The growth of the market has led to an increasing sophistication in its sale and consumption, with varieties such as 'Malawi Gold' famed worldwide for their quality.

In contrast to the early spread of cannabis throughout East and central Africa, there were no documented uses of cannabis in West Africa before the twentieth century. In West Africa the earliest mentions of cannabis, then known as *diamba*, *jamba* or Indian hemp (though now known as *igbo*, *wee* and *wee wee* in Nigeria and Ghana), are from the beginning of the twentieth century. According to Akyeampong, Sierra Leonean traders played a crucial role in the distribution of cannabis along the West African coast in the 1920s and 1930s.[47] Nigerian historical records on cannabis are rare for this period but confirm the central role of Sierra Leonean producers and traders at that time. The more widespread use and the beginnings of cultivation in West Africa can be attributed to the return of West African soldiers from South Asia after the Second World War. According to police reports of the 1950s, the hemp cases found were 'mostly seamen and others connected with ports' such as 'ex-servicemen and touts showing foreign seamen around'. Most of the cannabis was in transit, in particular coming from India and going to the UK, but some was also smoked by seamen and touts in Lagos. Since its post-war reintroduction, cannabis use expanded from a fringe habit to a widespread phenomenon among most social strata and regions. The psychiatrist Tolani Asuni, who treated patients using cannabis, observed that before the 1960s Indian hemp was mainly smoked by deviant social strata, such as ex-soldiers, ex-prisoners, prostitutes and urban unemployed. This perceived link between cannabis use and urban deviance at the time of the Nigerian nationalist movement resonates with Akyeampong's argument that cannabis, like locally distilled gin, was a symbol of deviant subcultures opposed to the colonial state in West Africa. Nevertheless, in the course of the 1960s cannabis use soon expanded to rural areas and other less marginal strata of society, such as students.

In Nigeria, by the end of the 1970s, cannabis had established itself as the nation's favourite illegal drug, in terms of use, cultivation and smuggling. The Nigerian civil war between 1967 and 1970 had given cannabis cultivation another strong impetus, as many soldiers started using the drug during the war, while use by musicians such as Fela Kuti further disseminated its consumption among wide segments of Nigerian society.[48] At the turn of the 1980s cannabis use had became so popularized that psychiatric doctors reported cannabis in more than half of the drug-related hospital admissions and twice as many as for alcohol. Police seizures of cannabis at the time reached figures that would only be surpassed in the 2000s. As Axel Klein states:

> the use of cannabis has simply entered the cultural mainstream with increasing numbers of users in the motor parks, at university campuses and in the bars and places of enjoyment in the cities.[49]

Western stereotypes of cannabis consumption can lead to erroneous notions of the nature of its use elsewhere in the world. Typically, cannabis is seen as a recreational drug in the West; however, in Africa – and in the Caribbean – much usage appears more 'functional'. As Laurent Laniel points out:

> users frequently report that it enables them to work harder at physically demanding jobs ... or at jobs that require staying awake for a long time, like driving, standing guard at roadblocks or houses, etc.; or to 'get courage' in order to perform tasks perceived as difficult or dangerous.[50]

For Laniel, recreational usage is more connected with those 'westernized' in their consumption habits.

While cannabis is illegal in Sub-Saharan Africa, African perceptions of cannabis are as polarized as those in the West between those who see it as a 'hard drug' strongly linked to madness,[51] and those who extol its virtues as a 'herb'. A clip available on YouTube shows a young Kenyan smoker differentiating cannabis from cocaine and heroin, and speaking of how it aids him in 'meditation'.[52] In Ghana, Henry Bernstein reports on young consumers who eloquently defend cannabis as 'life-enhancing: good for ailments (asthma, appetite loss), reading, contemplation and sense of self – and sexual potency'.[53] These same consumers were very much influenced in their perceptions of cannabis by reggae culture and Rastafarianism, which is a major factor throughout the continent. Both those merely enamoured of reggae music and those who are serious Rastafarians – or members of the Rastafarian-influenced brotherhood of the *Baye Faal* in Senegal – all tend to have highly positive views of cannabis and constitute many of its consumers.[54]

Opposing views emanate from more 'respectable' segments of society, and cannabis – like khat – frequently becomes conflated with 'harder' substances in media portrayals and in everyday discourse around drugs. Its use – and that of alcohol and other substances – is also strongly opposed by various Christian denominations. Even in contexts where cannabis has been smoked for centuries, its use by younger generations is frowned upon, and the common discourse that substance use has degenerated as a result of the loss of power by African elders can be heard, as reported by the 1999 UN report from Mozambique.[55]

MANDRAX AND METHAMPHETAMINE These two substances have a very involved history in South Africa, although uncommon in other Sub-Saharan African countries. Methaqualone – a drug originally synthesized in the 1950s in the quest for a new anti-malarial – is known more widely in Africa by the proprietary name of Mandrax. It is a sedative with similar effects to barbiturates and had a brief notoriety some decades ago in Europe and North America as a recreational drug. However, its use in South Africa – particularly among the so-called 'coloured' (mixed race) communities of such bleak urban zones as the Cape Flats – has no parallel in its scale, although some usage is reported in East Africa, a transit point in the journey of Mandrax from Indian and Chinese laboratories to South Africa.[56] This sedative was produced and marketed legally until 1977, when reports of its widespread recreational use led to prohibition. Demand and production to feed it have remained strong and with Ted Leggett estimating that about half the Mandrax used in South Africa is manufactured abroad, there is a substantial amount of home-produced product, often manufactured using what is termed 'bucket chemistry'; it is relatively simple to produce given the right precursor chemicals.[57] It is sold in pill form, with distinctive branding similar to that used by producers of ecstasy.

Nowadays, it is used by some to help in coming down from the effects of crack cocaine, but for most of its users it is one of the two ingredients in the 'white pipe' – homemade pipes improvised from the broken-off neck of a glass bottle. Although recreational consumption once involved swallowing it in pill form in combination with alcohol, the white pipe soon emerged as some innovator tried smoking the crushed tablets and adding cannabis (often a particular low-quality grade called *majat*, said to be dried using paraffin, which potentially adds to its intoxicating effects). This combination is potent, and Leggett describes it thus:

> The white pipe experience is an intense one. The initial rush is so powerful that many users 'ert' or 'earth' immediately after use – they lose consciousness of their surroundings and fall to the ground, drooling. This total loss of control means that Mandrax can only be smoked among trusted companions, which reinforces the social nature of the drug. Once the rush is over, intoxication and sedation continue for a period of time dependent on the quality and quantity of the drug consumed. The experience is highly addictive.[58]

Mandrax's popularity in South Africa is linked to the country's isolation in the time of Apartheid, as South Africa's drug cultures developed along their own trajectories with little influence from abroad. Indeed, some blame Apartheid more directly for the spread of Mandrax and other drug consumption, through the details of a top-secret project in the late days of Apartheid that emerged in the Truth and Reconciliation Commission. The project to research possible biological and chemical weapons stockpiled large amounts of Mandrax and other drugs, many of which allegedly ended up entering the illegal market, fuelling suspicion that drug abuse was being spread among the black and 'coloured' population to disrupt anti-government activity.[59]

Whatever the truth of the Apartheid's regime's involvement with Mandrax and other substances, it is clear that Mandrax came to play a huge role in the economy and culture of South Africa's gangs, some such as Cape Town's 'Americans' earning huge sums from its trade. Post-Apartheid, things have changed, and the white pipe and Mandrax in general appear to be being supplanted by other drugs – notably crack cocaine, and the newest drug on the South African block: methamphetamine, known there as *tik*. Methamphetamine (also known as 'crystal meth' elsewhere in the world) is a potent form of amphetamine that has been around for over a century, yet only gained its great notoriety in the last two decades. Its potency combined with its relatively low retail price has made it both dangerous and accessible. While amphetamines differ chemically from cocaine, they have a similar effect in increasing dopamine levels, and in causing an initial rush followed by a much longer-lasting high. It therefore gives plenty of 'bang for the buck', and is regarded as 'poor man's cocaine'.[60] Experiments and personal testimony by consumers suggest it can easily induce dependence, causing intense cravings for repeated doses. As with other drugs, some consumers appear more susceptible to becoming dependent on methamphetamine than others. It is sold in the form of purified crystals that are injected, snorted or smoked. The last of these is the most common method used in South Africa, and the name *tik* comes from the sound made by the crystals when heated in homemade pipes made from old light bulbs in which it is smoked. Smoking it gives its consumers an intense rush of euphoria and energy (and increased libido), and some consumers are said to stay awake for days on end through prolonged usage, eventually succumbing to the need for sleep (sometimes induced by using the white pipe). Horror stories abound in the media and online of this new menace, described by one Cape Town anti-drug activist whose own family has been deeply affected by the drug as 'the worst drug that ever did hit Cape Town'.[61] This is quite a statement, given what other substances have been consumed there, and echoes the way methamphetamine was spoken about in the US in the early 2000s, where it was routinely described as 'worse than crack' (crack cocaine being infused with such a dangerous reputation that it had become a benchmark with which other substances could be compared).[62]

The *tik* phenomenon began in the early 2000s, and the rapidity with which it has emerged has been astonishing. Leggett's seminal book *Rainbow Vice* (2002) on the South African drugs and sex industries didn't mention the substance at all; by the time Rodney Scholes was conducting research in Cape Town among drug users, it was the only substance people wanted to talk about, and had hit South Africa like a 'tsunami'.[63] Data (2008) from South Africa in the *WDR 2010* state that 6.9 per cent of young people of secondary/high school age surveyed reported ever having used amphetamine-like stimulants, which one can assume means methamphetamine.[64] That the substance was relatively easy and cheap to manufacture meant that it could be sold cheaply at retail (it is currently sold at around 15–30 rand, £1.50–3, for a small retail unit known as a 'straw'), and the accessibility of precursor chemicals such as ephedrine means there is no shortage of supply. The supply of these precursors owes much to a remarkable transnational barter economy of illicit goods, involving the exchange of ephedrine and a shellfish: the abalone (*Haliotis Midae*). This shellfish, found off the coast of South Africa, is in high demand in China, and Chinese syndicates (often described as 'Triads') exchange illegally poached abalone for ephedrine (and also the precursor chemicals for Mandrax). As Jonny Steinberg relates, 'Chinese businesses bartered cheaply acquired chemical precursors for high value abalone, while Western Cape drug lords bartered cheaply acquired abalone for high value drugs'.[65]

Like Mandrax, the *tik* economy is tied up with South Africa's gangs, and young members of the 'Americans' and their ilk seem to form a large proportion of its consumers. But they are not alone, and 2008 estimates report around 200,000 users in Cape Town alone, while 70 per cent of those under the age of 20 receiving treatment for problematic substance use were *tik* users.[66] The majority of its consumers appear to be mixed race, and typically are in their mid-20s.[67] As mentioned above, poverty and social exclusion cannot alone explain problematic drug use, and even in the case of *tik*, there are consumers from wealthier strata of South African society. However, the grim spread of this powerful substance and its hold on people on the margins of the 'Rainbow Nation' who feel as disenfranchised as ever, shows the very real way in which drugs and drug cultures can give meaning and purpose to people who feel an absence of them in other aspects of their lives. While youth from the affluent middle classes have embraced the 'club drugs' of an international 'rave culture' (ecstasy, LSD and so forth), drugs far too expensive for most users in the Cape Flats and elsewhere, the cheap and dangerous 'rush' and 'high' of *tik* offer (fleeting) pleasure and fellowship at a potentially high social cost.

HEROIN AND COCAINE Although heroin and cocaine are very different substances with different effects on the consumer – one being a depressant, the other a stimulant – we treat them together in this section as they were introduced to Africa at around the same time, and they are perceived as the classic 'hard drugs' both in Africa and more broadly. While cannabis is the most widely consumed drug on the continent, it is these two that make most of the headlines. Beyond Africa, this is because a number of African countries act as transit points in the trafficking of these substances to Europe and North America. However, the 'spillover' effect resulting from transnational trafficking means that many Africans have become consumers, causing rising concern in several countries. By 1999, cocaine (in the form of powder and as crack) and heroin use was reported in all ten countries covered by the *Drug Nexus in Africa* report.[68] While these substances are still associated with wealthier segments of society and with tourists in some countries, low prices have made them more accessible in poorer urban areas. There are few estimates of cocaine consumption in Africa as a whole, but for heroin, estimated ranges from the *WDR 2009* suggest that between 550,000 and 650,000 West Africans, 100,000 and 1,330,000 East Africans (a huge margin of error that shows how much guesswork is involved in these figures), and 230,000 and 310,000 southern Africans use opiates (heroin being the most common opiate drug). While these figures are unreliable – in particular, the figures for East Africa sound extraordinarily high, and Nigerian data have not been updated through new research for almost 15 years – they do reflect the increasing availability of these substances in the wake of Africa's emergence as a major trafficking hub.

Indeed, African consumption of these substances is very recent, although opiates such as laudanum were in the medical chests of explorers and missionaries, and morphine has been used in African hospitals for over a century. In fact, a shortage of morphine supply for Africans suffering pain is a major problem in itself, as 'fears of addiction, excessive bureaucracy, inadequate requisitioning and a reluctance to use oral morphine outside hospital are widespread in Africa'.[69] Cocaine is also reckoned to have been used recreationally in Kenya's 'Happy Valley' of hedonistic settlers. For East and West Africa, the introduction of these substances is generally dated to the 1980s, when increased efforts against traditional smuggling routes to Europe and North America led to an increase in the amounts smuggled through Africa. Greater vigilance also encouraged smugglers to divert some of their supplies to domestic markets as risks in smuggling increased. For example, Mombasa's port was and remains an important hub for drug trafficking, and it is from there that heroin use permeated first Mombasa itself, then smaller towns along the coast such as Kilifi and Malindi.[70] Nairobi itself was not immune to heroin, and the drug has a market there too.[71] There are also reports of cocaine supply and use in Nairobi, and two video reports available on YouTube purport to show the trade of cocaine there.[72] In Tanzania, too, heroin is now a cause of great concern, particularly in larger urban areas such as Arusha, Dar es Salaam and Zanzibar.[73] In Malindi – whose heroin problem is well studied thanks to the pioneering 'Omari Project', an NGO offering help to addicts in the area – there are claims that tourists introduced heroin to local Swahili youths working informally in the tourist industry. By 2000, researchers were able to estimate that there were 600 heroin users in Malindi, with a relatively low number of women users (around 30), in a population of about 100,000.[74] In Tanzania, Sheryl McCurdy links increasing injection of heroin to globalization: as more people travelled throughout the world, some picked up the habit in places such as Italy and Pakistan then brought it back with them.[75] She points out that the spread of heroin has much to do with changing fashions of consumption that owe a great deal to globalized drug culture. Susan Beckerleg and Gillian Hundt movingly convey the 'structural violence' of poverty, gender and dependency in Malindi for women heroin users.[76] The link of problematic heroin use and social exclusion – while not necessarily a causal link – is as pronounced in East Africa as it is elsewhere in the world.

In Nigeria, while use of these substances (heroin is known in Nigeria as *gbana,* and cocaine as *chanwe chunke*) was almost unknown in the 1970s, clinical evidence since the mid-1980s confirms their increased use. In 1989, 40 per cent of patients entered southern Nigerian drug treatment facilities for heroin use and 14 per cent for cocaine use. Of total national drug-related admissions, 20 per cent were for heroin in the same year.[77] This differed starkly from the 1970s, when doctors reported the non-existence of any hospital admissions for these two drugs. Some ascribe this sudden rise of 'hard drug' use to Nigerians returning from spells abroad – often as students – who had acquired a habit elsewhere and had the funds to buy the substances from traffickers. 'Through the network of friends and circles of followers these habits soon spread to other sections of the urban community, where it retained a nimbus of sophistication.'[78] Hard drug problems at that stage were mainly the prerogative of the wealthier classes, which, as Klein points out, had great repercussions as it was on these wealthy individuals whom resources had been spent on education,

43

and on whom responsibility had been showered in employment back home.[79] As with cannabis, sailors – who sometimes have the opportunity to indulge in such substances in their travels – have been considered a vector for the introduction of heroin and cocaine into Nigeria. Whoever introduced them, by the early 1990s and probably earlier, heroin was no longer just confined to the wealthy, and Klein describes vividly the use of heroin in 'joints' in a slum neighbourhood near Lagos where male and a small proportion of female customers came to smoke powdered heroin from home-made hubbly-bubbly pipes, paying what were relatively large amounts of money in such an area.[80]

In South Africa the key date for the introduction of heroin and cocaine appears to have been 1994 and the ending of Apartheid. After this date, movement into the country was much less restricted, and heroin and crack cocaine were supposedly introduced by an influx of Nigerians. While the vast majority of Nigerians in South Africa are professionals engaged in legitimate pursuits, those involved in the drugs trade have helped generate a stereotype of Nigerians, one fuelled by high levels of xenophobia. The main appeal of South Africa for Nigerian traffickers was its potential as a staging post for onward transit of drugs to Europe, but some also took advantage of a developing local market, introducing substances that had been a 'non-issue' in South Africa before 1994.[81] Crack cocaine – a smokeable form of cocaine that offers a more rapid and intense high than powdered cocaine at cheaper cost – caught on quickly in deprived areas of major cities, such as Johannesburg's Hillbrow area, home to some infamous 'crack houses' and known as 'Little Lagos' for its thousands of Nigerian residents who arrived post-1994.[82] One such crack house was featured in a documentary from the early 2000s, and had sophisticated CCTV equipment to monitor who accessed the building, and reinforced steel doors to hinder the potential entry of police. An old lady sat in the entrance hall supplying clients with the substance and the paraphernalia used to consume it (pipes made from bulbs and wire mesh on which the crack is melted prior to smoking). Like elsewhere in the world, crack cocaine consumption is intertwined with the sex industry, and many sex workers develop serious habits. Desperation for crack has apparently led to a reduction in the money sex workers charge for their services as they are so keen to make any money they can, while some agree to engage in risky condom-free sex for the sake of obtaining the substance. According to Leggett, South African sex workers have been encouraged by suppliers to introduce crack to their clients, so spreading its consumption further afield. The spread of crack and that of heroin in South Africa are interrelated, as crack users after heavy consumption often use depressants to 'come down', and while such drugs as Rohypnol can fulfil this function, heroin appears more effective. Historically, drug usage in South Africa has divided up along racial lines, with cocaine and heroin mainly associated with white consumers. However, as data from the South African Community Epidemiology Network on Drug Use (SACENDU) make clear, their use by Indians, 'coloureds' and 'blacks' is growing.

There appears to be some difference in the social status of heroin and cocaine consumers between East Africa and Nigeria, a difference created by pricing. In Nigeria, these substances, though still cheap by international standards, were more expensive than cannabis, restricting their use, although a lack of recent research on pricing means that it is difficult to be sure of the current situation. In Kenya, however, heroin (known by some as *unga*, the Kiswahili word for flour) can be bought for around Ksh100–200 (roughly £0.80–1.60) a *kikete* (a small wrap of powder, enough for a dose). Of course, even at that relatively low price, a habit can become expensive, especially given the high rates of poverty in the area. Indeed, one study of drug use in Zanzibar suggests that injecting drug users spend around the equivalent of US$246 a month on heroin, a staggering figure given Tanzania's per capita income of $330 in 2005.[83] Earning sufficient money often means 'engaging in illegal and other high risk behaviours such as sex work, theft, and selling drugs'.[84]

Perhaps the most critical factor in relation to the use of heroin (and to a lesser degree, cocaine) is their mode of consumption.

While initial consumption of heroin took the form of 'chasing the dragon' (inhaling the vapours generated by heating heroin powder on foil), and some consumers prefer to smoke heroin in tobacco or cannabis cigarettes, consumption through injection is becoming more and more prevalent, especially in East Africa. Until recently, it was thought that African heroin users were generally averse to injecting as the mode of delivery, preferring to smoke it instead. On the East African coast, some researchers link this change in consumption method with the import of a new type of heroin from 1998 – 'White Crest' – that could not be 'chased', but could be injected.[85] Injecting is far from universal among heroin consumers in East Africa: in Malindi most new consumers begin by smoking, some later making the transition to injecting, and researchers estimated that 50 per cent of users were injectors in 2000. Injecting drug use (IDU) is not limited to East Africa, and as well as increasing prevalence in West Africa, there are reports of IDU being 'prevalent even among refugees from the interior regions of the Democratic Republic of Congo'.[86]

Of course, the switch to injecting comes with serious health risks, not just from the dangers of overdose or adulterated product, but also those of blood-borne infections such as hepatitis C and HIV. The connection of such infections with IDU is of course well known, and was one of the main concerns about IDU in the UK in the 1980s in the midst of a potential HIV epidemic. In fact, the UK's Advisory Council on the Misuse of Drugs then supported the approach known as 'harm reduction' on the 'basis that HIV posed a greater threat to society than drug use itself'.[87] While HIV's spread was less severe than feared in the UK, clearly the well-known high rates of HIV in Sub-Saharan Africa suggest that the risk of transmission through IDU is serious. Data in this regard are rather sparse, but what there is suggests there is real cause for concern: in Zanzibar, HIV prevalence is 28 per cent among those practising IDU who share needles; in Dar es Salaam, there is an estimated prevalence of 57 per cent among the same. In Mauritius – where there is a long history of opiate use – there is a very high rate of needle sharing in IDU with a consequent high rate of HIV infection: '92% of new HIV infections in 2005 were identified' in those practising IDU.[88] Not all such users share needles, and there is awareness of the risks in doing so, but many still engage in this risky practice. The cost of needles and the stigma of accessing them means that many reuse and share their current ones. Some even report the practice of 'flashblooding' whereby a drug user injects him or herself with the drug, then draws back blood into the syringe which another user then injects to feel some of the effects.[89] This is mainly practised by women in Dar es Salaam, where those who have made enough money to buy heroin provide this 'flashblood' for friends without the money for a full hit.

Harm reduction measures including the provision of clean needles and syringes are fairly common in the West, and evidence strongly suggests their effectiveness in curbing the spread of HIV, as research from Australia demonstrates.[90] However, current policy in Africa discourages needle exchange programmes and other such harm reduction measures. The focus of drug policy has been firmly on criminalization rather than treatment, with pressure from donors such as the US preventing harm reduction measures being applied through the fear of condoning drug use.[91] However, there is hope that this might be changing, and US policy outlined in the US President's Emergency Plan for AIDS Relief announced in July 2010[92] now promotes the use of sterile needles and syringes. This policy change has also occurred in Kenya, where the head of the country's National AIDS and Sexually Transmitted Infections Control Programme announced in August 2010 that needle exchange would now be a legitimate part of policy.[93] How effectively such a policy will translate into action remains to be seen, but this development does give grounds for cautious optimism.

Consumption and crisis

From the licit to the illicit, Africa has a wide variety of stimulating and intoxicating substances to offer, each with their own histories and cultures of consumption. Indigenous substances including khat, kola and fermented beverages have been joined over the centuries by cannabis and tobacco, and, much more recently, by the likes of heroin, methamphetamine and cocaine. Consumption of psychoactive substances in Africa is thus not just a function of Africa's recent role as *entrepôt* for the hard drugs trade, but an age-old practice that is just as ingrained into society as elsewhere in the world. However, further qualitative and quantitative research is needed to properly assess trends and patterns in consumption. Psychoactive substances go in and out of fashion, and their cultures of consumption can also change, as the incorporation of khat into a global youth culture and of cannabis into a globalized Rastafarian culture make clear.

But should we be alarmed by apparent recent rises in consumption of such substances? How much harm is being wreaked on African societies by drugs? Aside from the lack of data to convincingly show that per capita drug use in Africa is rising, one should be cautious when generalizing about their harms: substances such as khat and cannabis have been consumed for centuries in Africa, and while patterns have changed and elders lament their growing use by youth, their consumption poses a relatively low risk. The war on drugs rhetoric that holds sway at this moment in history builds on the notion that all drug use is inherently problematic, and so assumes that if a 'drug' is being used, harm is occurring. But this is clearly not necessarily so. Indeed, one of the biggest risks for their consumers derives from the illegality of cannabis and the varied legal status of khat: the risk of arrest and the social harms this can cause. Of course, the more recently introduced 'hard drugs' have more harm potential for the health of their consumers, and the social health of communities. The growing public outcry over their use in such affected areas as the Cape Flats and Kenya's Coast Province reflect genuine concern, especially where little funding is provided for facilities to help problematic users. These are often either too expensive or non-existent. Rather than specialized treatment centres, problem users often end up in psychiatric wards. Such users fall by the wayside in the present climate of punitive policy towards drug use imported from the West (see Chapter 4). Clearly resources need to be directed towards effective policies to help such consumers, whether *tik* users in the Cape Flats or heroin users in Malindi. Making true headway with problematic drug use among such marginalized communities requires addressing the wider problem of their marginalization and the structural violence they often encounter in their lives, and this is an enormous undertaking.

While harder drugs steal the headlines, the most commonly used substances by Africans will remain licit caffeinated substances as well as tobacco and alcohol. Even cannabis – despite its ubiquity throughout the continent – is unlikely to match their popularity. Being licit does not equate to being free from harm of course, and alcohol and tobacco pose far greater risks to Africans than the likes of heroin through the far greater scale of their consumption. No psychoactive substance – licit or illicit – is entirely unproblematic; of course, substances categorized as 'drugs' are not necessarily wholly problematic either, and this holds true for their impact on development in Africa too, as the next chapter will argue.

2 | Drugs and development: a new threat or opportunity?

> Drug abuse furthers socio-economic and political instability, it undermines sustainable development, and it hampers efforts to reduce poverty and crime. (Jan Kavan, president of the United Nations General Assembly, 2003)[1]

Drugs are not usually discussed in the context of African economic development, unless serving as symbols for economic decline, crisis and state collapse. This chapter assesses the links between drugs and development in Africa. In recent years UN research has begun to explore the links between crime, drugs and development, claiming that drug consumption, trafficking and associated crimes such as corruption contribute to underdevelopment. This chapter actively engages with this body of recent official research and challenges some of its key assumptions, proposing a more nuanced understanding of the economic impact of drugs. In particular, as agricultural crops and trading commodities, drugs have provided farmers and entrepreneurs with opportunities not readily available in the difficult economic environments of many African countries. Thus, it needs to be asked whether drugs are necessarily a threat to Africa's development or if the markets for certain substances can be seen in a more positive light.

Received wisdom

For over half a century, African countries have seen a wealth of projects designed to increase their social and economic well-being through 'development', from state-managed economies in Ethiopia and Tanzania, import substitution industrialization, through the embrace of market fundamentalism under structural adjustment programmes, to the championing of migrant remittances. Few of these schemes have proved effective, and several have been singularly ineffective in fulfilling the stated aims of 'development', now summarized in the form of the Millennium Development Goals. These are the range of targets agreed upon in 2000 that were to be met by 2015: ending poverty and hunger; achieving universal education; increasing gender equality; improving child health; lowering rates of maternal mortality and improving reproductive health; fighting HIV/AIDS; enhancing environmental sustainability; and bringing about a global partnership with improved trade terms and debt relief for developing countries.[2]

Within this historical context, growing attention is now paid to drugs as a development issue. Drugs, corruption and crime go together, so we are told, destabilizing societies, reducing productivity and thus impeding development. Such is the received wisdom commonly seen in reports and conferences under the aegis of the UNODC. Indeed, the former head of the UNODC – Antonio Maria Costa – lamented in an opinion piece in the *Guardian* in 2008 how 'the cocaine used in Europe passes through impoverished countries in west Africa, where the drugs trade is causing untold misery, corruption, violence and instability'.[3] And this is not just a matter of concern for the effects on developing countries, but also of concern for ramifications back in the West. The growing 'securitization' of development in the wake of the attacks of September 11 means that overseas aid spending is now often justified to the public as essential for security at home.[4] Also, improving economic conditions in countries now seen as *entrepôts* for the drugs trade is viewed as a way to cut off drug networks that thrive on underdevelopment, and so reduce supply to western countries. Thus, the increasingly strong link between drugs and development is not merely rooted in concern for the economic and social welfare of developing countries, but is also connected to more parochial western concerns.

Whatever the reason for the increasing attention given to drugs and development, the link between them emerges in several different aspects of their trade and use. Merrill Singer, an anthropologist, has studied the negative impact of drugs upon developing countries in depth. He focuses on both legal and illegal substances – strongly highlighting the malign effects of tobacco in the developing world – and divides up their impacts into the following categories:[5]

1 Productivity – Singer draws attention to how drugs can impact negatively a country's productivity on both the supply side – through injuries and health problems acquired in processing drugs, and through arrests of low-level employees in the drugs trade – and also on the use side, where health problems can reduce productivity of workers. Singer cites research that shows drug users have more accidents at work and are absent much more often. A critical factor is the spread of HIV/AIDS through drug use, which can deplete a workforce (see below).

2 Threat to youth – youth are always considered most at risk from drugs, as the previous chapter mentioned in regard to Africa. For children and youth to consume drugs is considered both dangerous and a waste of their potential and productivity. Singer relates the special threat to street children, whose numbers have been swollen so markedly 'as a result of widespread poverty, urban migration, and breakdowns in the social service sector following structural adjustment'. [6] Drug use (particularly of solvents) among street children is a worldwide phenomenon, and Singer cites examples from India and Cambodia. As well as the health risks of consumption, there is concern for child labour in the production and trade of drugs. Children from poor families are far more likely to become involved in this labour, as research from Brazil demonstrates. Through drug use and involvement in their trade, children's education can be severely affected. Older youth in poverty-stricken regions are also considered at risk of involvement in the drugs trade through a lack of employment alternatives. The cultural cachet and 'cool' that sometimes surround drugs and their trade can also prove enticing for youth, a globalized phenomenon found in developed and developing countries.

3 Health problems – as we saw in the previous chapter, risks of blood-borne disease contagion are very great among IDUs, and rates of HIV/AIDS can be very high among such users in developing countries. Sub-Saharan Africa is not alone in this respect, and Singer draws examples from Bangkok where HIV prevalence among IDUs stands at 40 per cent. Of course, different substances are associated with a range of harms, all of which can potentially add extra stresses to households and communities, especially where healthcare provision is lacking.

4 Corruption and the breakdown of social institutions – examples of the linkages of the drug trade and corruption are very easy to find. Pablo Escobar's 'silver or lead' approach is perhaps one of the most well known, where officials and others were offered gifts and money in return for favours, and threatened with death in return for resistance; parts of Mexico are now beset by similar corrupting influences of drugs traffickers. To quote Singer:

[d]rug-related corruption ... not only involves the bribing of government officials to turn a blind eye to drug-related activities or to actively aid them, it also involves ensnaring law enforcement representatives to provide cover for the movement and street sales of illicit substances.[7]

Thus, such public servants – often poorly remunerated in developing countries – and the institutions they represent become further corrupted and undermined. Ban Ki-moon, secretary-general of the UN, argues that:

it is the world's vulnerable who suffer 'first and worst' by corruption such as the theft of public money or foreign aid for private gain. The result ... is fewer resources to fund the building of infrastructure such as schools, hospitals and roads.[8]

Meanwhile the income spent on drugs and the stresses that arise from arrests and health problems can tear apart families, rendering it 'even more difficult to survive in a globalizing world'.[9]

Drugs and development

5 Violence – one only has to think of Colombia's recent history, as well as the tragically high rate of drug-related deaths in Mexico, to realize the horror that can come with the trade in these high-value illicit commodities. Singer also relates the horrors that are associated with drugs in Jamaica and Haiti, as 'cartels' seek to maintain power against rival groups and law enforcement. History also provides the opium war as an example of conflict over the drugs trade, while consumption of psychoactive substances including alcohol is often associated with volatility and violence. Clearly such violence – whether at a societal or individual level – can destabilize regions, creating barren ground for economic and social development.

6 Environmental degradation – to Singer's list, one might add the environmental damage often associated with the production of drugs, including the leaking of hazardous pesticides and other chemicals into the ecosystem, and deforestation as a result of cocaine production or cannabis cultivation. Such damage can have severe ramifications for people's immediate health, as well as the long-term consequence of dwindling natural resources.

Most examples used in discussions of the topic are drawn from places with such troubled relationship with drugs as Colombia and Afghanistan, as well as the Caribbean and elsewhere. Certainly, the drugs trade has played a huge role in the destabilization of these regions – though how much of that is down to the drugs themselves and how much to drug policy is a question to which we return below. But what of Africa? What examples that fit the above categories are cited in the African context?

Regarding productivity, discourse around psychoactive substances in Africa often laments the waste of working hours through recreational usage of stimulants and intoxicants. Alcohol is often implicated in this, as is khat. Indeed, in the case of khat, long chewing sessions in the Horn of Africa and elsewhere are seen by many observers as examples of indolence that undermine a work ethic. However, the impact of drugs on food security is seen as a greater threat. On a continent where hunger is a recurrent concern, the use of land to grow drug crops is seen by many as immoral and irresponsible. In regard to cannabis, the INCB report of 2003 spoke thus: a 'worrisome development appears to be the increasing shift from cultivation of food crops to cannabis in some areas [of Africa], resulting in food shortages'.[10] A cable sent from the US embassy in Freetown to Washington – and leaked through Wikileaks – speaks of the concern with which Sierra Leone authorities view increased cannabis production, seeing it as a major threat to food security.[11]

Most concern about drugs in Africa, as elsewhere in the world, revolves around the young. As we saw in the previous chapter, there is great fear of an 'epidemic' of drug use among young Africans. Drugs such as khat have a certain cachet among the young as 'cool', while youthful alcohol use is reckoned to be increasing rapidly too. The use of solvents is particularly high among street children, while education rates are said to suffer through child labour in the production of drugs such as khat. The high rates of unemployment throughout the continent, from the Cape Flats to Dar es Salaam, also create fertile environments for the spread of drug use among marginalized youth, further damaging their prospects of employment.

The harm drugs can cause to health is also a key concern, especially considering the link with the spread of blood-borne viruses such as HIV discussed in the previous chapter. The high rates of HIV/AIDS mean that IDU is especially dangerous on the continent, as research from East Africa in particular has shown. A whole range of health damage is associated with drug use in Africa, from the relatively minor (poor dental hygiene, for example) to the major (fatalities from overdose).

Poor remuneration for police officers and other officials makes them very susceptible to bribes, and there are many cases of suspected drug-related corruption on the continent. Corrupt figures in government are also implicated in the trade, as such people are said to offer protection to drug traffickers. This is especially associated with Guinea-Bissau – as we will see later in the book – where such infiltration of the state by traffickers generated the fear that the country was at risk of becoming a 'narco-state'. Such concerns have been felt in Kenya too, in the wake of accusations against certain members of parliament that they have been corrupted by drug cartels, facilitating shipments of cocaine in return.[12]

In writings about Africa, drugs are also depicted as endangering the foundations of society through instigating and perpetuating violence. The use of cannabis among combatants in West and central Africa is well attested, and many claim that such usage increases their courage and stamina levels.[13] More importantly, drugs are often mentioned as 'conflict goods', helping 'warlords' fund militias.[14] To quote the INCB report of 2003 once more:

> Information gathered from war-torn countries in Western and Central Africa, in particular in the Central African Republic, Côte d'Ivoire and Liberia, indicates that the arms and ammunitions used by rebel groups and criminal organizations to destabilize those sub-regions may have been partly procured with the proceeds of illegal drug trafficking.[15]

The use of khat was similarly linked to conflict in Somalia at the time of the country's collapse in the late 1980s/early 1990s.[16]

The risk to the environment in cultivating drug crops is also commented upon in the African context. The illegality of cannabis means that it is often grown hidden among forests, sometimes resulting in the destruction of large areas of indigenous forest, as shown in the Mount Kenya region by aerial photographs from 1999.[17] Khat cultivation is also associated with forest destruction, for example in Ethiopia.[18] There are also concerns about the use of pesticide in khat cultivation, and overuse of irrigation to water the crop. In Somaliland, there is a saying 'cut a tree to chew a twig' that suggests that demand for khat leads to increasing felling of trees in rangelands to make charcoal and thus raise funds.[19]

These themes reflect real dangers and potential dangers for Africans; however, it must be emphasized that a detrimental effect of drugs and development in Africa has nowhere been demonstrated through sound research. In fact, there has been little exploration of causality in all the hand-wringing about drugs impeding development. There are no data presented to support arguments of drug-related economic decline, nor any solid evidence that development would progress apace were it not for drugs. Also, there is little evidence beyond hearsay to support a straightforward causal link between trade and use of drugs and such conflict as that which has engulfed Somalia.

The most compelling case for a large-scale negative impact of drugs on development is surely that connected with their smuggling and the connected criminality and corruption. But even here it is unclear whether the drugs trade has corrupted states such as Guinea-Bissau, when the criminality and corruption of the state pre-dated Africa's recent absorption into the international drugs trade (see Chapter 4). Furthermore, any impact that drugs have in impeding development and generating corruption begs the question of whether it is the drugs themselves or drug *policy* that is the culprit. As Singer states for developing countries in general:

[I]n many developing countries the War on Drugs has undercut civil liberties and human rights, strengthened the armed forces in countries with a history of harsh military rule, supported militarization of local police forces, spread the use of torture by law enforcement, provided support to powerful leaders who are themselves heavily implicated in the drug trade, contributed to a significant social conflict and political instability, and undercut the livelihood of impoverished people without providing them with alternative means of making a living.[20]

Disaggregating the effects of drugs and that of the War on Drugs is not something attempted in a concerted manner by the UNODC or the INCB, although the UNODC has recently acknowledged the 'unintended consequences of drug control', 'the most formidable of which is the creation of a lucrative black market for controlled substances, and the violence and corruption it generates'.[21] Less

likely to be acknowledged soon is the potential for a more positive appraisal of the impact of drugs and development. Are drugs
necessarily a threat to Africa's economic growth and well-being?
Or have they offered opportunities for improved livelihoods? To
address these questions, we examine the production of Africa's
two major drug crops – cannabis and khat – which the received
wisdom would certainly suggest are major threats.

'Green gold' and the 'cow of the ground': Africa's drug crops

Globally drug crops have become a key economic resource
for many farmers, and persuading – or forcing – those on the
margins of the world economy to give up such important sources
of livelihoods has proved extremely difficult, whether in regard to
coca farmers in South America or opium farmers in Afghanistan.
Singer describes well the 'paradox for development initiatives'
posed by drugs, that despite their potentially negative impact
on societies listed above, they provide poor households with
opportunities in several parts of the world:

> Opium, for example, is the biggest employer in Afghanistan
> ... Similarly, in South America, the cocaine trade attracted
> thousands of families fleeing extreme poverty in other locations
> to coca growing areas, coca being perhaps the only cultigen
> they could make a living from in a region in which the soil is
> not well suited to intensive agriculture. Among poor farming
> families in Myanmar, Grund ... notes that growing opium pop-
> pies 'pays for what most people in developed countries take
> for granted'. In the words of one Myanmar man, 'Opium is our
> food, our cloths, our medicine, the education of our children.'[22]

Similarly, in Africa, drug crops are also entwined with livelihoods.
Not all these crops are illegal. In fact, many African drug crops
are 'respectable' and traded legally throughout the world: tea,
coffee, kola and tobacco being good examples, while the production of alcoholic drinks – whether legally or illegally – is a major
source of income at both a local and national level. However,
in this chapter we focus on two in particular, one illegal – can-

nabis – and one legal in its main producer countries, but illegal in many other countries around the world, and internationally frowned upon – khat. Both offer good examples of how illegal and 'quasi-legal' crops can fill gaps left by a faltering market for more 'respectable' cash crops, and both elicit praise in this respect from farmers: in the Nyambene Hills of Kenya where much khat is grown, it is dubbed 'green gold', while farmers in Lesotho praise cannabis as the 'cow of the ground'.[23]

Cannabis Including North Africa as well as Sub-Saharan Africa, the UNODC estimates that cannabis is grown in at least 43 of the continent's countries, and that Africa accounted for 25 per cent of global cannabis production in 2005.[24] North Africa – and Morocco in particular – is where much of the world's cannabis resin is produced, while cannabis herb has proved a remarkably successful crop in Sub-Saharan Africa, with varieties such as Durban Poison and Malawi Gold being much in demand internationally; domestic demand is high no matter what the variety. As mentioned in the last chapter, cannabis has a long history in Africa, especially in East and southern Africa: its use is no recent phenomenon, and nor is its cultivation. While thorough research into its early production is still very much lacking, there are tantalizing clues in the chronicles of early explorers documented by Fabian (see Chapter 1), and even in the form of a photograph of a 1930s cannabis plant growing on a compound in the then Bechuanaland, modern-day Botswana (captioned as 'for private use'), found among the photographs of Isaac Schapera.[25] An expanding cash economy no doubt generated some commoditization of cannabis even before its illegality, although the current boom in production owes much to the rise in value accruing to cannabis thanks to illegality.

Cannabis production was almost certainly commonplace throughout the continent by the mid-twentieth century; however, commentators consider the critical time period for an expansion of its production to be the 1980s onwards. The 1970s and 1980s were times of economic crisis and structural adjustment in much of Africa. Rising oil prices and declining terms of trade for export crops such as cocoa or coffee, combined with economic misman-agement led to an array of structural adjustment policies across the continent, which were marked by painful liberal economic reforms and a further deepening of the economic crisis. Some of the hallmarks of liberal adjustment policies were the devaluation of African currencies, the reduction of the state bureaucracy as well as cuts to welfare provisions. These policies would be imple-mented differently across the continent and at different times, but in most cases they negatively impinged on large sections of African society.[26] The removal of trade barriers imposed under structural adjustment led to further crisis, as home-produced maize, rice and other crops faced competition from cheaper imports. This agricultural crisis was compounded by ecological degradation in several regions and the effects of drought. It is in this context that cannabis appeared as a 'compensation crop'.[27] The UNODC provides a clear case study of the link between falling legitimate commodity prices and a rise in cannabis production from Côte d'Ivoire. Farmers interviewed generally began cultivating the crop quite recently in the wake of the dip in cocoa and coffee prices, and the economic logic to do so was impeccable:

> Prices recorded in the south-west in 1995 showed that the annual production of 0.1 hectare of cannabis sold wholesale at the farm gate earned as much as the output of 30 to 40 hectares (15 to 16 tonnes) of cocoa. In other words, cannabis brings 300 to 400 times more revenue than cocoa, and for much less work, in the Ivorian agricultural sector.[28]

Pierre-Arnaud Chouvy and Laurent Laniel describe a boom in the cannabis economy following the introduction of structural adjustment programmes as living conditions became more of a struggle and conflicts proliferated, both factors they link to increased demand for cannabis. This hypothesized rise in demand and falling commodity prices spurred more farmers to produce a crop with many advantages:

> Because cannabis can adapt to a wide range of environmental

settings, even to degraded or naturally poor quality soil, it may be grown on lands unsuitable for other crops. Given this 'performance,' it may be integrated into agricultural production systems practically regardless of the agro and economic criteria normally governing them, namely access to [fertile] land, capital and workforce. This means that cannabis cultivation is accessible to a wide range of farmers and, under present conditions, it seems to be imposing itself as an alternative crop of prime importance in West Africa as well as in Central Africa and Southern Africa.[29]

Cannabis plants are also easy to grow among other crops, so allowing the plants to be easily hidden. In western Kenya much cannabis is said to grow among plantations of sugar cane, and as it is also often grown on very marginal land, its cultivation is not necessarily incompatible with the production of subsistence crops. Furthermore, the crop requires little input either of fertilizer and pesticide, or of labour. Of course, these advantages of cannabis as a cash crop would have little worth for farmers were it not in demand and marketable. Indeed, what little research there is on cannabis in Africa shows how developed local, regional and global markets are for the commodity. As Henry Bernstein shows for Ghana, cannabis grown in the country is sold in Ghana itself, in neighbouring countries, in Angola and as far afield as Europe.[30]

What case studies there are concerning the cultivation of cannabis in Africa certainly support the notion that cannabis is acting as a 'compensation crop'. In the case of the small mountainous kingdom of Lesotho – one of the few African countries where significant research on cannabis production has been conducted – an increase in cannabis production is very much linked to a decline in wage-labour, high demand for cannabis in surrounding South Africa, and a landscape degraded by soil erosion caused in part by overgrazing. Lesotho has been a key labour reserve for South Africa, and 200,000 men found employment in South Africa in the 1970s, mainly in the mining sector.[31] This would have been a large proportion of the population, which even today is only just over 2 million.[32] The migration patterns of Basotho – the people of Lesotho – men meant that remittances were a key part of the Lesotho economy, helping many in the rural areas. With increasing retrenchment in the 1990s following a fall in gold prices, among other factors,[33] remittances have decreased, and cannabis has filled the resultant gap in income for many Basotho, especially those in the rural areas, where it is now a major cash crop. In fact, for the country as a whole, cannabis is a major source of foreign revenue, and 'while there is no official data, other than police seizure statistics, all observers with knowledge of rural livelihoods in Lesotho agree that cannabis is the nation's most significant cash crop'.[34]

Cannabis has been an important cash crop since at least the 1980s, although the extent of its importance only became more widely appreciated after a survey of villages to be flooded by the Mohale dam in the 1990s, where cannabis was found to account for 60 per cent of arable crop revenue for the villagers. This led to some dilemmas about how to compensate farmers for lost revenue from an illegal crop.[35] Cannabis is grown in all regions of this mountainous country, including on small plots in the capital Maseru, '[h]owever, the main growing regions are found in the high mountain zones in the centre and east of the country, as well as in the western foothill region'.[36] Basotho distinguish between several qualities of cannabis, with certain regions associated with certain types: the long history of production and usage in the region ensure that there is much in-depth knowledge of the crop. The crop is mainly grown by smallholders, often intercropped with maize, although there are reports of larger-scale mono-cropping of cannabis on farms of around 3–5 hectares in area.[37] Cannabis is planted between mid-August to mid-October in Lesotho, providing a first harvest of inferior product – apparently consisting of the male plants – in January, and the main harvest from February to April.[38] Most work on the crop is done by members of the household, although harvest can be a communal occasion with work parties enlisted to help. Farmers simply dry the crop and pack it into sacks, while some add extra value to their crop by preparing it into rolled cigarettes.[39]

Lesotho is well integrated into a regional network of cannabis supply, with much of the crop destined for South Africa and some re-exported to Europe. While technically illegal in Lesotho, the importance of the crop for farmers and the economy as a whole means that it enjoys a 'de facto decriminalization' as few politicians and law enforcers have the will to curb its cultivation, and many themselves benefit from its trade through actual involvement and bribes to 'turn a blind eye' (a theme we will return to in Chapter 4). Thus, Lesotho offers a perfect political as well as ecological environment for the production of cannabis, and South African traffickers are happy to exploit this fact.

Profits from cannabis are much higher further along the commodity chain – as traffickers boost its value to account for their risk – however, it still offers farmers much higher returns than other crops. In the late 1990s, profits from a hectare of cannabis were estimated at 20 times that for maize.[40] In Julian Bloomer's more recent research in a Lesotho village called Botsoapa, cannabis was still the most reliable crop in the current economic climate, although prices fluctuate, and so profits are not guaranteed. Prices drop rapidly at harvest time due to the glut of the crop entering the market; thus, poorer farmers with little option but to sell the harvest straight away fare badly compared with those who can store their harvest until prices rise once more.[41] Bloomer found that in Botsoapa, approximately 28 per cent of annual income derived from cannabis, though few farmers get rich from growing it, and, indeed, it was the poorer farmers who relied more on the crop; wealthier ones gained a higher proportion of income from non-farm income. Still, cannabis cultivation 'has offered the opportunity of generating an income from the resources available to almost every household in Botsoapa, namely land'.[42]

A very similar situation exists in certain parts of rural South Africa, where cannabis has also been integrated into local and regional economies. This is the case in Pondoland in the Eastern Cape where large quantities have been produced for decades.[43] Such is the scale of cultivation and the renown of the product that there is 'cannabis tourism' to this region, although there is variety

63

in the extent of cultivation between villages and households. Kepe provides a case study of one Pondoland village – Mlanjeni – which is located in an especially well-regarded area for quality cannabis. Kepe distinguishes between three different types of growers (all of whom are male): (1) those who grow solely for their own consumption; (2) those smokers who sell their surplus crop; and (3) those who grow and trade the crop as a full-time occupation. Thembala Kepe found 13 of the third group in Mlanjeni, all of whom were married males with large families. Like the Basotho farmers, these growers are not generally wealthy, and Kepe emphasizes the discrepancy between the profit dealers make in the city per kilo (1,000 rand) and that made by the growers (40 rand) for the same amount. Growers often plant the crop deep within the surrounding forest, where soil is fertile and well watered, and where growers face less risk of being caught by police or meeting with the disapproval of other villagers. While growers in the area are rarely targeted by police, cannabis's illegality does encourage smaller operations. Kepe emphasizes that it is cannabis's illegality that keeps its value high, and suggests that were calls for its legalization – which are quite common in South Africa[44] – to meet with success then many livelihoods in villages such as Mlanjeni might be adversely affected.

Cannabis is firmly integrated into the economies of several other southern African countries, including Malawi, Swaziland and Mozambique, and one can imagine the economic context for farmers in these countries differs little from that in Lesotho and Pondoland. Given the international disapproval of cannabis, one might wonder how such farmers feel about growing such a crop, especially given the fact that economic pressure plays such a role in encouraging its production. As Peter Gastrow maintains, there is great ambivalence among farmers: while many would readily grow other crops, for others it is hard to understand why cannabis is illegal given that it has been used in some parts of Africa for centuries.[45] Also, given that the anti-cannabis laws come from national governments often considered predatory by the rural poor – and from international bodies of little moral standing among them – it is easy to see how farmers are unlikely to worry about the morality of growing such a crop (another theme we reprise in Chapter 4). Furthermore, as Gastrow points out, the movement in many western countries to dilute the illegality of cannabis through decriminalization of small quantities of cannabis, or legalizing its use for medical treatment as in several states in the US, raises important questions for countries where it has become a significant source of livelihood:

> If the demand in such [western] countries is not kept in check by governments, but is allowed to increase, should the police in poor and least developed countries, where cannabis is indigenous, has been used for centuries and is grown by many to survive, be expected to use their scarce resources to fight against its supply?[46]

Such frustration is evident in the lament of several African representatives at a meeting on drugs and Africa that there was a:

> lack of support and action by donor countries and organizations [in regard to cannabis] and [they] appealed for the establishment of alternative development cooperation programmes targeting illicit cannabis plant cultivation in Africa ... and in the provision of support to farmers. It was noted that, in Africa, weak economies had responded to the demand for illicit drugs from developed countries.[47]

Even in the unlikely scenario that the international will were found to fund crop substitution trials of cannabis for other crops, experience from elsewhere in the world suggests these will be hard to implement successfully. Similar trials in Afghanistan, South America and elsewhere have run into several problems. As summarized by Francisco Thoumi, these include the difficulties in finding crops of similar value and stability of price, and the ability of traffickers to raise prices in response to crop substitution to make the illicit crop more attractive.[48] In the case of cannabis, finding substitute crops that would fare as well on the degraded soils that cannabis can adapt to will prove very tricky indeed, as will persuading African farmers that cannabis is as harmful as campaigners in the war on drugs maintain. Given the integration of cannabis into many rural livelihood strategies, it is highly unlikely that its production could be curbed, no matter how concerted the efforts to do so. As Chouvy and Laniel make clear, the 'development of cannabis cultivation in Sub-Saharan Africa is more a consequence of the continent's economic, political and ecological problems than one of its causes', and the only way to reverse this trend would be through addressing the structural causes of poverty.[49]

Khat International bemusement and concern for the increasing production of khat are well illustrated by the following anecdote: when Irish businessman David McKernan – boss of a coffee shop chain – revisited a village in the Ethiopian region of Harar where he had attempted to instigate a water project, he was horrified to see fields of his beloved coffee replaced by fields of khat. In an article in the Irish *Independent*, farmers were said to obtain four times as much for khat harvests compared with coffee, yet McKernan could not feel anything but indignation that such cold economic logic could cause a switch from one stimulant drug to another.[50] McKernan's reaction is typical of many commentators on the preference of many farmers in Ethiopia, Kenya and Yemen to switch from coffee and its falling prices to khat, a crop that continues to offer them a better livelihood.

Khat has for centuries been cultivated in Hararge province in Ethiopia, while cultivation in Kenya's Nyambene Hills also dates back at least 150 years and most likely more. Alongside much of northern Yemen, these three growing zones are those most associated with the crop, and those where it is grown most intensively. Worries about the supposed negative effects of khat upon society have long been present in its growing regions, and its history in Kenya is illustrative of the debates that come to revolve around such crops.[51] There its increasing consumption in the lowlands of northern Kenya caused panic among colonial officers worried about its corrupting influence on local pastoralists. The khat they were consuming was coming from the Nyambene Hills north-east of Mount Kenya, a district inhabited by the Meru, Bantu-speaking agriculturalists. Unlike other cash crops introduced by settlers, khat was an indigenous crop commercialized by Africans,[52] and the colonial authorities were taken aback when they finally researched the trade and realized how far Nyambene khat was travelling. By the late 1940s, it was already being exported as far as Dodoma in Tanganyika, although the bulk of the exports were to Isiolo – a town of great importance in the history of the Kenyan khat trade easily accessible from the Nyambenes – and to Nairobi. Improved transport infrastructure and growing urbanization were both key factors in the spread of demand for the perishable commodity.

At first, concern about the health dangers of khat consumption won out, especially after the publication of a rather sensationalized special issue of the *East African Medical Journal* on the substance was published in 1945. This issue – though based on a very tenuous evidence base – gave those campaigning against it the weapon they needed to push for control. The feeling among the administration resembled that expressed by J. D. Rankine, the chief secretary, in a letter dated 22 January 1948, who said he considered khat:

> a very serious danger to the health of Africans in this country and no feelings that we are damaging a paying trade should prevent us from stamping on it as hard and often as we can.[53]

Attempts to control the substance's consumption in the colony through a permit system and an outright prohibition in the north were trialled. Among other absurdities, the permit system only allowed consumers certified as 'addicts' the right to consume khat, as the administration thought they might 'die' without their fix of this relatively mild stimulant. This led to thousands of consumers throughout Kenya self-declaring themselves as addicts in order to be allowed their chew.

Meanwhile Meru producers and traders were lobbying hard on behalf of the trade, stating how important the commodity had become for them both economically and culturally. With such lobbying and the obvious unworkability of the legislation, colonial officers in the most intensive production area of Meru district, while initially suspicious of the crop, soon came to see its worth for the economic development of the region. Having abandoned attempts at control except in the north, by the late 1950s, the colonial administration instead attempted to regulate and rationalize its production and trade through standardization and an aborted attempt to create a cooperative system for the commodity. There was even talk among district officers about promoting the export of Kenyan khat to other consuming hotspots such as Aden in competition with Ethiopian and Yemeni khat. While exuberance on behalf of the late colonial administration to promote the export of Meru khat abroad faded in the face of increasing international anxiety about khat consumption, production continued to grow along with demand.

For much of the colonial era, Meru was the only district where khat was produced in great quantities, and the Meru had honed their expertise with the crop over centuries, creating a sophisticated intercropping system that prevented soil erosion and protected other crops.[54] Furthermore, alongside Arabs and Somalis – who have been involved in the trade in Kenyan khat for many decades – the Meru innovated much in regard to marketing. The varying qualities and types of khat – distinguished by growing region, variety of tree, age of tree, part of the tree harvested, length of the stems etc. – allowed it to be marketed for both wealthy and poor consumers, thus expanding its consumer base.

Some colonial interference aside, Kenyan khat has received little in the way of government assistance, farmers and traders being left to their own devices. While not daring to antagonize farmers and traders, since independence the Kenyan authorities have applied a policy of not encouraging, but not discouraging, production of a crop that was bringing in substantial council revenue through tax and foreign exchange earnings with growing trade to Somalia (much of the Kenyan crop departs for Kismayu, Mogadishu and other Somali towns and cities). Paul Goldsmith describes the further spurs to production in the Nyambenes provided by the spread of the Somali diaspora in the wake of its civil war of the late 1980s and early 1990s.[55] Now Kenyan khat is sent as far afield as the UK (legally) and North America (illegally), and new areas of cultivation in the Nyambenes have been opened up to satisfy this demand. Lack of official involvement in the trade means that accurate quantitative data are lacking, but by the early 2000s the most quoted figure was that the khat trade was bringing in $250 million a year to the Nyambenes. Indeed, rather than negatively affecting food security, such relatively high income levels have helped make the region more food secure in recent times than nearby districts where the dominant cash crops are tea, coffee and cotton.[56] Certainly the 2002 tonnes of Nyambene khat imported to the UK alone each year are indicative of the scale of production and importance of this crop for Kenya.[57] In the Nyambenes, farmers have constantly emphasized to researchers how much more valuable this crop is for them than more 'respectable' crops such as coffee, while income comes not only from its farming but also from its trade, as Meru are highly involved in its national retail trade and transport, while also entering into the international export business alongside Somalis, whose dominance of the international trade has been the source of some rancour among Meru.[58] Khat's cultural resonance for the Meru of the Nyambenes (see Chapter 1) has been enhanced and reinforced greatly by its economic worth to the district: it is so integrated into culture and economy, that schools and churches in the region often have a few khat trees to help support themselves financially. In the Nyambenes, few see khat as a dangerous drug menacing society (although there is concern at the use of child labour in the harvesting of the crop) but as the bedrock of the local economy; adults who praise khat for helping to send them through school are not hard to find. Earnings from the trade are not restricted to the Meru but also spread to the thousands of Somali wholesalers and retailers – many female – scattered throughout northern Kenya and Somalia.

While many commentators lament the waste of household

income in consuming what many see as a frivolous and dangerous luxury, as a crop and trade commodity khat plays an important role in generating wealth in Kenya. So much so that new areas of production are opening up in Kenya: several other areas of highland Kenya now produce a popular cheap variety called *mugoka*. A decade ago, this variety was scarcely known outside of a few select locations, but now is one of the most consumed types of khat in Nairobi, giving competition to the Nyambene product. Also, the fertile slopes of Mount Marsabit in northern Kenya are now being planted with more and more khat. A process of sedentarization has led to many formerly nomadic pastoralists growing crops in this area, and khat appears king at present. On Marsabit, farmers on marginal lower-lying land find it able to thrive where maize has failed. Furthermore, the huge popularity of khat chewing in the town and its environs means that demand is high, and it provides a decent supplement to income from pastoralism and other crops, as well as waged work in the town.

The Kenyan government's policy of neither encouraging nor discouraging khat production is one that is also followed in Ethiopia, where the lament that khat is taking the place of coffee is most commonly heard, and much anguished hand-wringing over khat's developmental impact has taken place. Ezekiel Gebissa has written the fullest account of the growth of khat production in Ethiopia, especially in the Harerge highlands, also known for fine coffee. When coffee prices became increasingly volatile in the 1950s, planting khat as a cash crop became increasingly common, encouraged by the growth of both national and international demand, and the building of infrastructure such as the Djibouti railway. Khat's perishability was no longer a barrier to its trade.

From the 1970s onwards, khat began to give coffee more and more competition as the primary cash crop in Harerge, and the scale of khat production continues to increase, and has spread far beyond the Harerge region. Data from 2007–08 – although likely to be underestimated, as 'national figures tend to understate the land devoted to growing khat, apparently to avoid criticisms for an unrestrained growth of a crop many consider a deleterious drug'[59] – state that khat is grown nationally on 163,227 hectares of land, an increase of 10 per cent on the previous year.

It is this continuing rise in production that raises so much concern, and the arguments concerning khat's developmental impact are very familiar from Kenya, and, indeed, resonate with the concerns about cannabis more widely:

> Critics maintain that the high proportion of prime agricultural land devoted to the cultivation of khat, the amount of productive agricultural labor wasted on chew sessions, and the huge household expenditure on the leaves have retarded the country's economic development. They argue that khat obstructs the officially promulgated policy of greater national self-sufficiency in food production ...[60]

However, as Gebissa points out, the increasing cultivation of a high-value cash crop such as khat makes perfect economic sense, especially in the Harerge context where population pressure has led to a rapid diminution in the average farm size, and a consequent inability of households to support themselves through subsistence crops or cash crops that fetch lower prices. Research continues to show lucidly the economic logic that encourages farmers to switch to khat, as per hectare cash income for khat growers is three times that of cereal growers, and:

> there is consensus among scholars that khat, as a cash crop, has had a positive impact on the quality of life of producers, traders, and others who earn their income from activities connected to khat.[61]

Khat farmers, according to Gebissa, are quick to point out the benefits they derive from the crop, although some are wary of just how sustainable the khat boom will be. Still, 'the majority of farmers benefited from the high price of their khat, the only commodity whose price kept ahead of inflation', while research shows that – similar to the situation in the Nyambenes – khat has allowed producers to ride out economic shocks, and remain relatively food secure while improving their standard of living.[62]

71

Khat growers earn around five times more cash crop income than non-khat growers, while owning more livestock, farm implements and other such indicators.[63] In fact, contrary to the anxiety over food security, the ability to feed children appears to increase proportionally with the amount of land dedicated to khat, and decrease with that dedicated to growing cereal crops.

Indeed, a far more positive gloss can be placed on khat's role in the economies of Ethiopia and Kenya's Nyambene district than given by development experts. As Gebissa reports for Ethiopia, khat farmers have been increasingly able to divert income from-khat into off-farm occupation, including transport, trade and retail sectors, allowing for migration to businesses in urban centres:

> Without any kind of extension support from the government, Harerge's farmers have shown that agricultural intensification and diversification are a great insurance against the inherent risks of subsistence farming for those who remain in the agricultural sector. By using the cash resources they obtained from khat sales to move to economic activities not connected to the smallholder agriculture based on meager and declining agricultural resources, they have shown what Ethiopia's Agricultural Development Led Industrialization (ADLI) strategy, a policy response to the country's food security and agricultural productivity challenge, should mean in practice.[64]

The story of khat's role in development does not end in the main producer countries of Kenya and Ethiopia, however, it also now extends to growing production regions in Uganda, as well as northern Madagascar. Indeed, in describing the expanding importance of khat production in several regions of Uganda, Susan Beckerleg makes similar points concerning the positive role khat can play in improving rural livelihoods. So important is this indigenously developed crop, that she even goes as far as to state that khat is subversive to international development practices, many predicated on the role of the outside developmental agency:

> Khat is subversive because in East Africa it has improved

the lives of millions of poor people who are not part of development programs. Khat, I contend, renders 'development' irrelevant to the lives and livelihoods of independent-minded producers and entrepreneurs.[65]

Furthermore, while khat is more often perceived negatively in countries such as Somaliland and Djibouti, where khat is consumed but not produced, as opposed to those where it is a significant source of foreign exchange and rural livelihoods, even in such countries khat is an important feature of the economy. Importers, transporters and retailers all benefit from the crop, as do the governments who impose tax on imports and trade.

Of course, one should not paint too rosy a picture of the crop. While khat trees can play an important role in preventing soil erosion and land degradation, such aspects of its production as child labour in Kenya are sources of concern. Also, as Christopher Clapham observes, it would be foolish to 'extol the crop as a potential basis for any broader process of sustainable development' given the lessons of other crops whose boom years came to a very quick end.[66] But as part of a diversified economy – and as part of an intercropping system that still allows the growth of subsistence crops as in the Nyambenes – khat production has had a generally positive impact on rural livelihoods.

Risky livelihoods? Thus, the support cannabis and khat provide to rural and urban livelihoods throughout Africa suggests that they can be assessed in a much more positive way than conventional wisdom would allow. However, how sustainable are these livelihoods linked to internationally reviled crops? Clearly, there are risks associated with cannabis and khat: vulnerability to law enforcement; little recourse to legal protection, certainly in the case of cannabis, although khat's legality in producer countries affords some protection in this respect; given cannabis's high value is supported by its illegality, future decriminalization measures may in fact harm rural livelihoods; the trade networks that farmers rely on to sell their crops at decent prices are vulnerable to closure by law enforcement agencies; there is also vulnerability to change in demand, legal status and so forth, as well as competition from other growing areas (for example, new khat-production areas are emerging, while much cannabis consumed in Europe is 'home-grown' with hydroponic technology, rather than imported). The dangers of reliance on khat have been demonstrated in recent months by the decision of the Dutch government to ban the commodity.[67] Many tonnes of Kenyan khat had been arriving there each week for the past decade, and so the impact back in Kenya – especially among farmers who have been specializing in growing the commodity for the Dutch market – is likely to be significant. There are rumours too that the UK – which imports even more Kenyan khat than the Netherlands – may follow suit rather than be isolated from its European partners, most of whom have now banned it. Given such risks and changing situations, would farmers be better placed eschewing khat and cannabis and sticking with either subsistence crops or legal cash crops?

The decision to grow such crops must be placed in the context of a lack of alternatives. As we have seen, land pressure and degradation means that hardy, tolerant crops such as khat and cannabis are sometimes the only ones that might thrive and provide an income that allows food security and some economic advancement. Also, there are many risks in all cash crops, even internationally approved ones that are very much at the mercy of global markets, as well as drought, pests and lack of agricultural subsidies to help provide fertilizer and other such inputs. Furthermore, the argument that cannabis and khat take away land that could be better used for food crops is an argument that would apply to other non-food cash crops such as tea, coffee and the vast quantities of flowers grown and exported globally from countries such as Kenya. In fact, cannabis and khat might allow more subsistence agriculture than 'legitimate' cash crops: cannabis does not require cultivation on the most fertile land – unlike other cash crops – and so can leave such land for food, while many farmers in East Africa intercrop other crops with khat, allowing a diversified approach to sustainable livelihoods.

Of course, even the risk of arrest or having one's crop of cannabis destroyed is low in many parts of rural Africa, where the power of the state is often too weak to reach farmers (see Chapter 4) and too constrained by a lack of willpower in tackling a crop so fundamental to many livelihoods. As mentioned earlier, figures of authority are also often implicated in the trade networks emanating out of production zones, and so have a vested interest in protecting farmers. In a rational assessment of which crop to produce, therefore, illegality – and the risk of future illegality – is for many farmers just not that critical a factor. Certainly, as experience elsewhere in the world shows, until viable alternatives are found upon which livelihoods can be based, internationally suspect crops such as cannabis and khat will continue to be farmed. As many African leaders have realized, international political will to combat the production of such crops in Africa is lacking, in contrast to the will to combat smuggling routes bringing harder drugs into Europe and North America. The current political and economic state of affairs – as well as the fact that khat and cannabis are often culturally validated in Africa – means that such crops are likely to remain significant factors in rural livelihoods for the foreseeable future.

Productive consumption

However, a more positive assessment of the role of cannabis and khat in rural livelihoods does not mean that other aspects of their trade and, in particular, their increasing consumption, are not having a far more negative effect on African society and economic development. One could view the situation faced by cannabis and khat farmers sympathetically while still disapproving of the crops they produce. Surely these commodities, so associated with idleness, unproductive leisure and social disruption, cannot be anything but harmful to society? However, might one have a different approach to the consumption of such substances – one that does not view their consumption as necessarily anti-development or the first step on the path to addiction? Examining drug consumption from a crude economic perspective that focuses mainly on lost working hours, or through the prism of public health, where the risks of consumption are always to the fore, is likely to lead to a jaundiced view of such substances and their potential 'anti-development' impact. In this respect, a dose of an anthropological perspective might help as something of an antidote to the truisms surrounding drugs.

While 'public health' perspectives rarely focus on positives of drug or alcohol consumption, anthropology has been accused of focusing on them too much. In the 1980s, anthropology was critiqued for its proneness to 'problem deflation' in respect to 'drinking problems in the tribal and village cultures under discussion', as 'functionalist' anthropologists portrayed consumption as socially integrative.[68] However, anthropology's close examination of patterns of sociality and culture connected with consumption patterns does allow for a much broader perspective than the general approach of 'public health' practitioners. Indeed, a close look at consumption patterns of cannabis and khat through anthropological and social historical perspectives reveals that they are not necessarily connected with idleness and unproductivity.

To begin with, the great demand that exists for these crops creates the economic opportunities that traders, farmers and transporters exploit. Also, as discussed in the previous chapter, consumption is not simply 'leisure'; Laniel emphasizes the functional use of cannabis throughout much of Africa, while the use of khat's stimulant effects in work contexts is well established. The use of beer as a reward for labour on farmland is another example of how stimulants and intoxicants can be consumed 'productively'.[69] From an anthropological perspective, even consumption in 'leisure' contexts is not simply 'unproductive'; Shelagh Weir's analysis of Yemeni khat consumption is most helpful in this respect, showing how mutual support networks are strengthened through khat parties, while news of job and business opportunities are shared.[70] Just as the sharing of food – 'commensality' – and gifts help bind people together, so does the sharing of cannabis, khat and other such substances; their consumption is productive of social ties. Consumption can also be highly creative, perhaps too much in the case of khat; so many ideas are supposed to flow from its consumption that consumers are said to 'build castles in the air'. However, the connection of khat consumption with poetry in Somalia, or cannabis with musicians throughout the continent, suggests another positive trait of their consumption.

All the above is not to deny the very real difficulties faced by African consumers of drugs – especially those using 'harder' drugs, and the many children dependent on solvents – or the way that drug consumption (khat and cannabis included) can break people apart as well as bring them together, so acting to curb development. However, it must be stressed that the impact of drugs upon development in the African context is far more complicated than the 'received wisdom' discussed above suggests. Certain 'drugs' can, in fact, be seen to play a positive role in rural livelihoods, and even in their consumption they are not necessarily the great hindrance to development that those wedded to the war on drugs maintain. Indeed, as more people and institutions question whether it is drugs or their prohibition that have the more devastating effects on society, it is time to also question the 'received wisdom' about drugs and development that helps maintain the hegemony of the war on drugs.[71]

3 | Drug barons, traffickers and mules: Africa as *entrepôt*

> Those who run trafficking operations are ruthless and often murderous. We must pursue them and thwart them with the full force of the law and international resolve. (Statement by Ban Ki-moon, UN secretary general, during a UN Security Council meeting on the threat of drug trafficking in Africa, 8 December 2009)[1]

On a sunny December morning in Nigeria's bustling commercial capital of Lagos, the streets crowded with cars and people on their way to work, a group of high-level law enforcement officials slowly made their way towards Apapa Wharf, West Africa's busiest port. They had just been informed of a large-scale seizure of heroin on a container ship arriving from Bangkok. At the port the officials were received by a group of US and Nigerian elite police officers who had made the seizure based on information provided by the US DEA. The officers proudly showed their superiors the packs of heroin hidden inside the freight. The smugglers had gone to great lengths to conceal the heroin in the interior of plastic water coolers.

A week later, on 23 December 1993, the same officers arrested the supposed mastermind behind this smuggling operation after he landed at Lagos international airport. Joe Brown Akubueze had taken the flight from Bangkok via Amsterdam to Lagos several times that year, most often to arrange the import of baby apparel and office equipment to be sold in south-eastern Nigeria's market town of Onitsha. In police custody, he admitted that he had personally packed the water coolers in a hotel room in Bangkok and that his business partner, whose name and whereabouts he had unsurprisingly forgotten, had provided the financial means for the smuggling operation. Akubueze described himself as a businessman who smuggled drugs because he had been struggling to support his family after a series of failed business ventures in the late 1980s. Based on the documents found in his possession, the officers discovered another container with smuggled heroin a few days later.[2] In total, Akubueze had helped to smuggle almost 250 kilograms of the drug to Nigeria, much of which would have been repackaged and smuggled by airborne couriers to the US.

Based on the exceptionally large amount of drugs seized, Joe Brown Akubueze became the archetypal African drug trafficker in public and media portrayals of the continent's drug trade. Twenty years after his arrest, he was still described as 'Nigeria's most renowned drug baron. He was very flashy, with sleek cars and [a] multi-billion naira empire spread across the country.'[3] In contrast, the lawyers preparing his prosecution at the time stated that he drove a very old car and was not a very wealthy man but rather an unsuccessful businessman.[4] Despite such divergent portrayals, Joe Brown Akubueze has remained among the prime examples of large-scale African drug trafficking and an early example of the bulk trade in drugs through the continent.[5] The arrests of drug entrepreneurs like Akubueze have helped to create the image of Africa as global drug *entrepôt*, although little is still known about these entrepreneurs.

Africa's image as a major drug transit point has emerged fairly recently. In the late 1970s international observers in the UN and US were still certain that the continent had no drug problem. A UN report about global drug trends in 1977 argued that 'Africa is still relatively free of major drug abuse problems'.[6] Ten years later this image had changed. Africa – in particular countries on its western coast – was perceived as deeply implicated in the transhipment trade in heroin and cocaine from Asian and Latin American producer regions to major consumption centres in the West. African criminals, such as Joe Brown Akubueze, were said to lead highly organized drug syndicates spreading across the whole globe. By 2005, the African transit trade in cocaine had

Africa as entrepôt

further expanded and led to UN descriptions of West Africa as the 'coke coast'. International experts have been certain about the ever-growing magnitude of Africa's role in the international drug trade. The head of the UN drugs agency recently argued in relation to cocaine in Africa, 'I have no doubt we're going to see production.'[7]

This chapter will critically examine Africa's emerging role as a drug *entrepôt* and challenge much of the related drug war rhetoric, which has promoted a largely ahistorical and stereotypical depiction of the continent and the drug trade. It will show that African entrepreneurs have had a well-established role in the international trade of various drugs long before the recent concern with African drug traffic. Even heroin and cocaine have been traded across the continent at least since the 1970s and this more recent trade has slowly expanded geographically and in terms of volume over the last 30 years. The reasons for the emergence and consolidation of the transit trade in heroin and cocaine are complex but essentially linked to global economic changes in drug markets and their control, as will be shown.

The chapter will argue that African drug trafficking is comparable to smuggling of drugs in other parts of the world. Smuggling operations are largely project based, profit driven and include a diversity of actors, and they have little in common with the 'cartels', 'mafias', 'drug barons' and the violence mentioned in official discourse. In fact, in the eyes of participants, such as Joe Brown Akubueze, the drug transhipment trade in heroin and cocaine is a means of economic diversification and perceived as a profitable business rather than just a crime. As Henry Bernstein has rightly argued, the drug trade has been one of the more flourishing trades across the continent in recent decades.[8] While this trade is set to increase in the coming years and decades, despite African and western control efforts, it is unlikely to grow unlimitedly and never into one of Africa's major foreign exchanges, as the continent's strategic position and comparative advantage in the heroin and cocaine traffic are not as favourable as presented in drug war discourse.

Africa in the history of the drug trade

Africans have long been important actors in the international trade in psychoactive substances. The continent's role in the history of the trade in drugs is likely as long as its history of drug consumption mentioned above. While many psychoactive substances used in its history were produced and used locally, such as fermented plantain wine or *pombe* in East Africa, many other drugs were transported from production zones to places of consumption covering vast distances on the continent and beyond.

The trade in kola and khat Some of these trades developed into extensive regional trading patterns, such as the trade in kola nuts in West Africa. As mentioned in Chapter 1, earliest records of this trade stem from the thirteenth century when caravans carried the precious nut from its production sites in the forest belt of present-day Sierra Leone, Liberia and Ghana across the sub-region and especially northwards into the savannah and Sahel. These caravans of kola were dominated by the merchants of the Mali Empire and carried the nuts across the Sahara as far as the Mediterranean. The Mali merchants traded not only in kola but a range of commodities, including gold, salt, slaves and textiles.[9]

Portuguese traders began to transport kola more extensively on their ships along the West African coast and in the nineteenth century the seaborne trade in kola expanded further and exports to Europe, the US and Brazil significantly increased. For instance, kola exports to England grew from a mere 56 tonnes in 1860 to 1,000 tonnes in 1910. Most of the 15,000 tonnes produced in West Africa at the time were nonetheless traded in the sub-region itself. While European colonialism accentuated the seaborne coastal and overseas traffic, the establishment of colonial state boundaries led to shifts in the interior trade routes and sites of kola production. Northern Nigeria's insatiable demand for kola, for instance, was to be satisfied by the growth of southern Nigerian production in the twentieth century. Although kola came to be produced and consumed ever more extensively, the long-distance kola trade across West Africa gradually vanished with the arrival of new state boundaries.[10]

The history of East Africa's khat trade has been portrayed as the reverse of the kola trade. Ezekiel Gebissa has argued that khat was largely traded locally until the twentieth-century construction of a colonial road and rail transport network that connected Ethiopian producers with the major consumer regions in present-day Somalia, Djibouti and on the Arab peninsula. Before the 1930s, khat produced in eastern Ethiopia was transported by headload or donkey-load to nearby towns. While occasional long-distance transport of khat existed, the perishable nature of the drug did not allow for the transport of khat for several weeks and months, as in the case of kola. Only after the road network extended to eastern Ethiopia's khat farms and the railways connected this part of the country to Somalia and Djibouti after the Second World War, did it become profitable for Somali traders to transport khat over longer distances. By the 1950s, Ethiopian khat had become the most popular variety among consumers in many parts of the Horn of Africa and even as far as in the British colony of Aden on the Arab peninsula. Gebissa argues that colonialism furthered the growth of the export trade in khat through the incorporation of Ethiopia into Italian East Africa between 1936 and 1941 and large investments in the transport infrastructure as well as the wartime embargo on Italy's colonies, which all contributed to the further economic integration of major khat producer and consumer areas.[11]

Kenya's history as a major *miraa* exporter was similarly limited by the drug's perishable nature and the 'need for speed' when transporting the bundles of khat from producers in Kenya's Meru district to consumers across the country, into bordering Somalia and through the Somali diaspora to the UK and US.[12] Until the producers of *miraa* were connected to the colony-wide network of roads and motorized transport in 1912, Kenyan khat could only travel two to three days as headload or on donkeys into nearby towns. By the 1920s, *miraa* traders already transported the bundles to major markets in Nairobi and on Kenya's coast and attracted the attention of colonial administrators, as described in detail in the previous chapter.[13] In the following decades the export trade to Somalia provided strong incentives for Meru khat production and some Kenyan–Somali border towns heavily depended on the trade and were described as the 'dying towns of the *miraa* trade' when a Somali import ban hindered trade from 1981 onwards.[14]

As mentioned in our discussion of khat's importance to development, Kenya's and Ethiopia's overseas exports have significantly risen in the last two decades due to improved and cheaper airborne transport to major centres of consumption among the diaspora in the UK and US. Somalia's collapse in the 1990s and the subsequent expansion of the Somali diaspora meant an increase in the planeloads of khat transported daily to London Heathrow and from there onwards to other parts of the world, particularly to the US. Kenyan and Ethiopian khat can today be bought for £3 a bundle in many Somali- or Ethiopian-run local shops in London, such as a *Costcutter* near King's Cross.[15]

The traffic in rum, brandy and gin Despite its links to Europe and the US, the ancient caravan trade in kola and the more recent commerce in khat remained principally regional trades, linking producers and consumers across Africa. Other psychoactive substances have been part of more extensive global trading patterns, such as the seaborne trade networks spanning the Atlantic.

The psychoactive substance most directly entwined with the century-long history of the Atlantic trade was alcohol. Rum and brandy were among the most important commodities shipped on the Atlantic to and from Africa, alongside cloth, ironware, guns and slaves. By the late seventeenth century European explorers reported the common use of imported French brandy and American rum at official or religious occasions across West Africa. Aside from the strong demand for the luxury alcoholic imports in African societies, the origins of the alcohol trade to Africa were in many ways linked to the transatlantic slave trade of the seventeenth and eighteenth centuries. While slaves were one of the major commodities leaving coastal areas of West and central Africa at the time, rum and brandy were among the goods imported. Slave traders at times even paid for slaves in the form of alcohol.[16] Nonetheless, the links between the export of slaves and the importation of 'harmful' liquor were not always as clear cut as in the portrayals of anti-slave trade and anti-liquor campaigners of the nineteenth century. As Philip Curtin has argued, the importance of the slave and alcohol trades varied geographically along the African coast and also over time. In places such as today's western Nigeria or the mouth of the Congo River, slaves were for long periods the major commodities traded, whereas in what is now Ghana, gold was far more important.[17]

In the second half of the nineteenth century, German and Dutch gin began to replace imported rum and brandy across West Africa. The rise of gin was driven by its lower cost and also the fact that it was available in smaller volumes. West Africans, many of who had benefited from the flourishing palm oil trade, could now afford to buy a few bottles of imported gin. Gin took on many functions and uses formerly reserved for brandy and rum, in particular as part of religious rituals and weddings, and it even acted as a currency, in particular in the Niger Delta. At the turn of the twentieth century many of the ships owned by big European merchant firms, such as John Holt, carried gin from Liverpool, Hamburg and Rotterdam to West Africa. In 1898 these trading houses trafficked an astounding 85,000 hectolitres of gin to West Africa and in the following years more than half of all the gin distilled in the Netherlands was shipped to West Africa. This clearly shows the importance of the West African market for European gin distillers and traders at the time.[18] In contrast, in East and South Africa, gin and the foreign liquor trade were never as significant, as their import and use by Africans was strictly prohibited.[19]

The relatively sudden rise in gin imports aggravated the anti-liquor movement, which saw cheap gin as endangering the health and well-being of Africans. The gin trade to West Africa was perceived as particularly immoral in the eyes of campaigners because many colonial governments in the sub-region derived significant revenues from taxing the trade. In some parts of today's Nigeria and Ghana, liquor taxes were the main revenue that financed the colonial project and led some officials to the realization that colonial regimes in the region were 'living on the proceeds of a grog shop'.[20] After many years of campaigning, anti-liquor activists succeeded in convincing colonial governments to restrict the gin trade to West Africa and introduce more stringent legislation. However, the main reasons why the trade started to decline from the 1920s onwards were limited shipping space during the world wars, as well as economic pressures felt by consumers during the 1930s depression.[21] Cheaper, locally distilled spirits and locally brewed beer after the Second World War became more important for West African consumers, although the region has remained an important market for European gin until today, with 5,000 to 7,000 hectolitres imported annually.[22]

It is also important to note that some of Africa's locally brewed beers have been successfully exported to other countries, such as Nigeria's *Star* beer, which is widely available across West Africa. More significantly, the African brewing giant South African Breweries Miller Ltd controls a large share of the American beer market since 2002 and this African takeover has led to campaigns against the consumption of 'non-American beer' in recent years.[23] These US campaigns against African-owned beer have been as unsuccessful as their equivalents a hundred years earlier in West Africa.

The cannabis trade While West Africa has had a long and important historical role in the Atlantic alcohol trade, eastern and southern Africa have also been long integrated into trade networks spanning the Indian Ocean. This is well illustrated with the cannabis trade. While the use of the drug among Arab communities in East Africa was first reported by European explorers in the eighteenth century, there is evidence that Arab traders had traded cannabis along the East African coast centuries earlier. Swahili traders from the East African coast are said to have transported cannabis further into the hinterland at least as far as the Great Lakes region.[24] In the second half of the nineteenth century, the use and trade of cannabis was given further impetus by the migration of Indian labourers to southern Africa. The British colonial authorities, having encouraged this labour migration, soon started to be concerned about the widespread use and trade of cannabis and the negative impact of the drug on the productivity of the Indian workforce as well as its spread to Africans, especially in the Natal colony. These concerns about cannabis arose despite the fact that the drug had been widely used and traded across southern and eastern Africa long before the arrival of Indian labourers. In 1923, the colonial government perceived the threat from the cannabis trade in Natal as so serious that it led to a request by the South African government to include the drug for first time in international control treaties – leading some observers to conclude that the origins of international cannabis control lie in Africa, thus challenging depictions of the continent's marginal role in the global political economy of drugs.[25]

The extent of the cannabis traffic was not comparable to the trade in other commodities across the Indian Ocean and within the sub-region, such as slaves, sugar or spices. However, the African–Asian cannabis nexus illustrates the close and long-established trade links of eastern and southern Africa with the Indian Ocean world. Only since the early 1990s has cannabis from the region become a major export commodity, now traded through the Atlantic route. UK court cases involving South African cannabis smugglers became frequent after South Africa was fully reintegrated into the world economy at the end of the Apartheid regime in 1994. Cannabis from South Africa, such as the well-known Durban Poison variety, is today transported by airborne couriers or in container ships to European consumers. In October 2001, Irish authorities seized a record 4-tonne shipment originating in Durban.[26] Also, in 2000 and 2001 law enforcers reported that the majority of cannabis seized in the UK came directly from South Africa.[27] While it is not known how much of southern Africa's cannabis is actually exported, as there has been little research on this issue, the volume of southern African cannabis exports is not destined to grow unlimitedly. Cannabis's bulky nature makes it easily detectable by law enforcement. There has also been a general trend in global cannabis markets to produce the drug closer to the centres of consumption; in particular, more potent cannabis is today produced in North America and Europe. African varieties, such as Durban Poison, are now also produced in consumer countries themselves.

To reflect on what has been said, Africa's role in the different trades in drugs has been of great importance historically. The trade in kola and khat has had long roots, spanned large parts of the continent and adjacent regions and also spread overseas more recently. The transatlantic alcohol trade had its peak in the colonial period but has remained important until today. The same is true for the trade in cannabis, which has been one of the many drugs shipped for centuries across the Indian Ocean and more recently onwards to Europe. Aside from these drugs, Africa has played a major role in many other drug trades, such as coffee and tea, which were popularized as export crops during the colonial period and have remained important export crops for many countries in eastern and western Africa. Countries such as Malawi and Tanzania have also played an important role in the export of tobacco to major European and American tobacco firms, as mentioned in Chapter 1. And African–Asian drug links have not solely been confined to khat and cannabis, as many of the prescription drugs available in African pharmacies and markets today are produced in China and India. This drug trade – about which far too little is known – is destined to expand as Asian prescription drugs are significantly cheaper than their African and western equivalents. Hence, while Africa's role in the international trades in drugs has been changing, it has remained a central actor.

The emerging heroin and cocaine connection

It is important to highlight these historical predecessors of today's heroin and cocaine trades as they not only reveal some of the roots of recent trading patterns but rectify an idea prevalent in official discourse that Africa's drug trade is a completely new phenomenon. The head of the UNODC for instance recently stated:

87

'Let's be frank: Africa in general, never faced a drug problem – whether we speak about production, trafficking or consumption. Now the threat is there, on all these fronts.'[28]

Such ahistorical views not only dramatize recent trends in Africa's drug markets but also hinder a better understanding of these trends. This section will show how long lasting even the heroin and cocaine trades through Africa have been and how they have changed over the last 30 years.

With Africa's long-term inclusion in global trading networks, the arrival of heroin and cocaine shipped through the region since the late 1970s should not have come as a surprise. Nonetheless, heroin and cocaine smuggling should not necessarily be seen as an extension or direct continuation of more historical trades in legal or illegal drugs, such as kola, khat or cannabis. This simplistic connection has at times been made by law enforcement officials, who have claimed that drug traffickers replaced one drug for another based on shifting seizures; for instance cannabis was replaced by heroin in the 1980s and in the 1990s there was a reverse to cannabis smuggling.[29] A few African smugglers might have traded heroin alongside cannabis or substituted one drug for the other; however, such instances are rare and not the norm. Law enforcement has made few arrests of cannabis smugglers who also smuggled heroin and cocaine. The way these drugs are sourced, smuggled and sold abroad is very different and it is difficult to imagine that cannabis smugglers are well qualified to smuggle cocaine. Instead, the commonalities between the different drug trades are their integration into larger international trading patterns that have spanned the Atlantic or Indian Ocean for centuries, patterns that have revolved around the commercial activities of entrepreneurs in the same trade centres, such as Lagos, Mombasa or Durban, and which have been affected by similar international and national economic forces, such as declining terms of trade for agricultural commodities and structural adjustment policies.

Our earliest records of the opiate and cocaine trade in Africa stem from the late nineteenth century, when the experimental production and export of opium along the Zambezi River, as well as coca cultivation in West Africa's botanical gardens, was promoted by colonial governments. Africa's colonial coca production remained a short-term trial, whereas Zambezi opium was successfully shipped to India from the 1880s onwards.[30] Nonetheless, with the onset of international drug control these colonial experiments with the African hard drug trade vanished at the turn of the twentieth century. Aside from a small-scale import trade in opiates and cocaine for medical purposes, Africa's heroin and cocaine connection only seriously manifested itself again in the course of the 1970s. During that decade a small number of African entrepreneurs, in particular from West Africa, started to diversify their businesses into the import and re-export of small amounts of heroin and cocaine. These entrepreneurs were the pioneers of the African transit trade and their number would grow from a handful into the hundreds over the 1980s.

The reasons for the emergence of Africa as a transit point for these drugs in the 1970s and 1980s are linked to shifts in the global markets for heroin and cocaine, as well as domestic circumstances that made the transit trade attractive to African entrepreneurs. On the one hand, global demand for heroin and cocaine as well as production increased significantly in the 1970s and led to the formation of relatively large and hierarchical drug smuggling organizations in the course of the 1980s, such as Pablo Escobar's Medellín cartel in Colombia. Growing demand and supply of drugs also caused more stringent enforcement responses in key producer and consumer countries, as well as along the major trade routes. The beginning of President Reagan's war on drugs in the mid-1980s accentuated these enforcement pressures on the global drug trade, particularly in the Americas. As a result, new and comparatively less risky transit hubs appeared far away from the traditional smuggling routes and the global heroin and cocaine trade slowly started to fragment, with a greater number of small-scale smuggling networks replacing large-scale organizations. These developments gave nascent African smuggling networks a competitive advantage over traditional smuggling operators.[31]

On the other hand, changed economic conditions in African countries also made the smuggling of heroin and cocaine more attractive, as they did in the case of drug production mentioned in Chapter 2. The 1970s and 1980s were times of economic crisis and structural adjustment across the continent. As discussed earlier, these policies would be implemented differently across the continent and at different times, but in most cases they negatively impinged on large sections of African society. The first African heroin and cocaine smugglers came from some of the groups most directly affected by these policies, such as the urban unemployed, students stranded abroad without state scholarships and traders of international goods. Hence, in the course of the 1980s, the small-scale trade in heroin and cocaine emerged as an alternative or as an addition to legal trades that had been negatively affected by economic crisis and structural adjustment.

By the 1990s, the transit trade in these two drugs began to consolidate itself and expanded from a few commercial centres, such as Lagos, to elsewhere in West and East Africa. West Africa's major economy of Nigeria, with its international trading centre of Lagos, remained the major way-station for the trade of heroin smuggled from India, Pakistan and Thailand and from Lagos onwards to the US. Cocaine was mainly imported from Brazil in the 1990s and after being repackaged it was smuggled onwards to Europe, particularly to the UK. For most of this period, overall seizures made in Lagos would amount to 200 kilograms a year and consisted of numerous 1–2 kilogram packs smuggled to consumer countries.[32] The 1993 seizure of Joe Brown Akubueze's 250 kilograms of heroin was in that sense atypical for seizures made in Lagos at the time but still in line with the relatively larger amounts imported to Africa from producer regions, as the risk of detection along the importation routes was relatively lower than along the route to consumer countries with their stringent enforcement policies. In aggregate terms, the seizures recorded along African smuggling routes and consequently the estimated volume of actual trade was still minor compared to the major smuggling routes from Asia and Latin America to consumer countries in Europe and North America. In 1996 for instance, heroin seizures on the whole African continent accounted for less than 1 per cent of global seizures.[33]

Apart from Lagos, other cities such as Dakar, Accra, Addis Ababa and Mombasa established themselves as African drug trading hubs in the 1990s and ever-new routes were developed to avoid law enforcement suspicion. Some of these new hubs appeared because Nigerian smugglers tried to dislocate the trade from Lagos, which already had a reputation for drug smuggling and a domestic drug war in the making. However, other African entrepreneurs also joined the profitable trade during this time and this led to a great increase in the drug smuggling routes crossing the continent.[34] Some of these routes were relatively new, such as the heroin route from Mumbai to Nairobi and onwards to the US. Some other routes, such as a recently discovered trans-Saharan cocaine smuggling route, drew on more ancient trading patterns that had been important to the trade in kola centuries earlier.[35]

In the second half of the 1990s the continent's most industrial-ized economy with extensive trading links to the world, South Africa, joined the African transit trade and became the continent's major consumer country of heroin and cocaine. As South Africa became fully reintegrated into the global economy with the end of Apartheid, so did the country's role in the international mar-kets for heroin and cocaine. It is commonly believed that West African drug smugglers first began to use South Africa as a transit point for the cocaine trade from the mid-1990s onwards and that locally based smuggling networks appeared in the follow-ing years. Mark Shaw's interview-based work with South Africa's heroin and cocaine smugglers showed that West Africans kept their dominant role in the transit trade through South Africa at least until the early 2000s.[36] In addition to its state-of-the-art transport infrastructure and trade connections, South Africa's role in the transit trade was driven by local demand in cocaine and heroin. As mentioned in our chapter on drug consumption, within a few years of heroin's and cocaine's greater availability, South African consumers had developed a taste for them and the country not only became a major transit point for these drugs but also the continent's major consumer country.

These significant changes in the African drug connection, which crystallized in the course of the 1990s, began to attract more international policy attention. Major UN programmes to study Africa's involvement in the drug trade appeared at the time and a variety of donor-funded projects were initiated to counter the continent's growing role as a supplier of heroin and cocaine to North America and Europe.

International initiatives to stop the supply from the continent, however, seem to have had little success in terms of dislocating the trade. Since 2005, larger-scale smuggling operations have become more widespread, as tonnes of Latin American cocaine have recently been shipped via West Africa to the burgeoning European cocaine market, where profits from the trade are still higher and the level of detection comparatively smaller than in the Americas (see Figure 3.1 for an illustration of the increasing cocaine seizures in the region since 2005). These smuggling operations – many of them led by Latin Americans or Europeans – have utilized new transit hubs, in particular Gambia, Guinea-Bissau and Guinea-Conakry. For instance, in January 2008 more than 2 tonnes of cocaine were seized by French police in a vessel off the coast of Liberia and in June 2010, Gambian authorities found more than 2 tonnes of cocaine hidden in a small fishing village. More established transit hubs have remained important in this new type of trade as well, as a reported cocaine seizure of 14.2 tonnes in Lagos in June 2006 shows.[37]

Estimates of the extent of this new type of smuggling, combined with the smaller-scale established trade, have been very diverse. Interpol estimates that approximately 300 tonnes of cocaine are annually shipped through West African ports and waters since 2005, whereas US authorities have claimed that slightly less, 245 tonnes, accounting for 70 per cent of Europe's annual consumption, passes through the region. In contrast, the UN estimates the volume of the West African cocaine trade much more modestly. In 2007 it claimed that about a quarter of cocaine consumed in

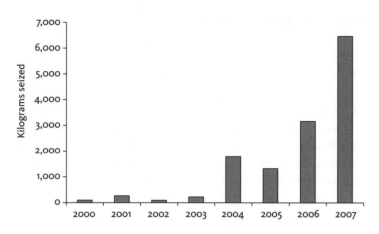

3.1 Annual cocaine seizures in West Africa (kilograms), 2000–07 (*source*: UNODC 2008, *Drug Trafficking as a Security Threat in West Africa*, Vienna: UNODC)

Europe, approximately 40 tonnes, with a wholesale value of $1.8 billion, transited through the region.[38] All these diverse assessments of the transit trade agree that the quantity of drugs transported through the region has generally increased during the second half of the 2000s. In any case, the great diversity of estimates on the regional cocaine trade also points to the underlying problem of the lack of reliable data on Africa's role in the drug trade – a problem already encountered in the context of African drug use and production in earlier chapters – and the heavy reliance on problematic seizure and arrest data, which indicate both shifts in the trade as well as changing efforts of law enforcement.

The lack of reliable data on the drug trade is only one major problem with official depictions of Africa's emerging role in the global trade in heroin and cocaine. As pointed out above, the second major problem is the neglect of the long and changing history of Africa's position in the trade. Several African commercial centres had been part of the trade for decades and new routes, such as the trans-Saharan cocaine route, were not invented by ingenious drug traffickers but merely drew on older trade routes across the continent.

Africa as entrepôt

93

Barons, traffickers and mules

The individuals and groups involved in smuggling heroin and cocaine have been as diverse as the trafficking routes crossing the African continent. Again, we know far too little about the different actors in the illegal drug trade and the following description of Africa's 'drug barons', traffickers and 'mules' is based on the available information about unsuccessful smugglers that have been caught by law enforcement as well as the few successful ones that have agreed to be interviewed by researchers. The UNODC official Antonio Mazitelli has provided the most systematic study on the organization of African drug smuggling based on his law enforcement experience in Africa. He distinguishes three broad structures of smuggling on the continent: 'freelancers', locally based smuggling networks and the foreign-led bulk trade.[39]

Aside from a few independent smugglers or 'freelancers', who finance, source and smuggle heroin and cocaine all by themselves, the great majority of drug smuggling through Africa has been conducted by local smuggling networks made up of three to a few dozen members. These networks transport tens or hundreds of kilograms of drugs by sea or by air from producer regions into Africa's commercial centres, as Joe Brown Akubueze did in 1993. They then repackage the drugs into smaller units – most frequently into condoms to be swallowed by airborne couriers – and have the drugs transported onwards to major consuming countries in very small quantities, ranging from a few grams to up to 2 kilograms. Aggregate volumes of heroin and cocaine smuggled in this way, based on available drug seizures, are comparatively small if compared to the smuggling of tonnes from major producer to consumer regions, for instance cocaine smuggled along the Caribbean route into the US market. However, the number of smugglers, in particular airborne couriers carrying drugs to the West, has been very large. This high number of arrested couriers has also attracted much law enforcement and media attention.

While these African drug trafficking networks are highly diverse, they share some common features, as they are relatively adaptable, project-based and comparatively small scale. As mentioned above, the smuggling routes used are highly fluid and can change from one consignment to the next depending on intelligence collected about the risk of law enforcement detection. Interviews with traffickers active in West and South Africa have also revealed the project-based nature of many smuggling operations, which means smuggling groups would only form themselves for a specific smuggling deal and disband soon after the profits were split. And while there have been some indications of smuggling operations involving more than 30 people, this does not seem to be the norm. Most African-based drug trafficking rings are relatively small, as they would involve less than a dozen individuals for each shipment and hence they are not comparable to the cartel-like formations of 1990s' Colombia.[40]

This adaptable, project-based and small-scale character is not restricted to African drug trafficking today but reflective of broader global changes in the drug trade. It has been common practice among law enforcers and the western press to argue that the flexible character of African drug trafficking is a reflection of the unique stateless past and entrepreneurial spirit prevalent among Africans, in particular some of its ethnic groups, such as south-eastern Nigeria's Igbos.[41] While some of Africa's drug trades have clearly been dominated by particular ethnic groups and nationalities, such as the largely Somali-controlled export of khat from Kenya to Somalia and Europe, in the case of heroin and cocaine transhipment there has been much more ethnic and national diversity of smugglers, although Nigerians clearly control an important share of the market. Besides, this argument neglects the fact that there has been a global trend towards more flexible, project-based and small-scale smuggling operations. Damian Zaitch in his ethnographic research on Colombian drug smugglers in the Netherlands has found that a similar type of loose network-based smuggling has become the norm since the second half of the 1990s. In the Colombian case the role of Escobar-like 'drug barons' and 'cartels' controlling large parts of the cocaine traffic has been replaced with more adaptable and smaller drug trafficking operations involving fewer people.

Africa as entrepôt

Hence, the lack of well-known 'drug barons' and large 'cartels' in Africa is also a representation of these global trends in cocaine and heroin markets.

As in the Colombian case, smuggling of heroin and cocaine involves a variety of roles that can be likened to legal trading patterns.[42] Drug smuggling groups encountered in Africa usually include:

1 Financial sponsor/s
2 Main coordinator
3 Couriers
4 Recipient in importing country
5 Money launderer
6 Settled law enforcer

Financial sponsors provide the funds to pay for drugs and couriers and they often have contacts abroad. A main coordinator of operations recruits couriers and organizes logistical aspects, such as flights and accommodation. In Zaitch's case, smugglers would have to raise around £10,000–20,000 to smuggle 5–10 kilograms of cocaine.[43] This amount of capital is needed to purchase drugs, hire couriers, arrange flights and accommodation and is not too dissimilar in the case of African drug smuggling, although little exact information exists on this. In any case, sponsors and coordinators come closest to what is characterized as a 'drug baron' or 'drug lord' in the drug war discourse, although these terms should be seen as obvious misrepresentations, as sponsors or coordinators rarely hold such powers over other network members as implied by these terms, and as in the case of Joe Brown Akubueze, they are rarely as flamboyant as press portrayals suggest. Sponsors and coordinators merely occupy a critical role within smuggling networks, as they provide the necessary capital, contacts and expertise for the smuggling to work.

Couriers or 'mules' engage in the most risky part of the work. Good couriers are not usually from the poorest sections of society but have some experience of international travelling, a valid visa and possibly a foreign passport that does not attract too much law enforcement attention. In the second half of the 1990s, South African nationals were among the preferred couriers for West African networks, as law enforcement did not yet suspect South Africa's role in the trade.[44] Couriers' personal financial situations also need to be hopeless enough so that they perceive carrying drugs as an acceptable risk. They receive on average between £1,000 and £5,000 per trip. While many couriers claim to be tricked into carrying drugs upon arrest, the majority are well aware of the freight they are carrying and most of the risks they take. Thus, the term 'mule' – someone being tricked or unknowingly taking a risk – should also be considered a misnomer in this respect.

In the importing country, a member of the network sometimes called a 'base' receives and pays couriers and sells the drugs. An additional network member comes to the consumer country independently after the sale of drugs and goes shopping for sponsors and organizers. In law enforcement discourse this would be referred to as money laundering. Furthermore, a bribed law enforcement officer can make a smuggling operation less risky and can provide important intelligence for the smugglers, although many operations also succeed without protection from corrupted law enforcement.[45] The roles of sponsor, coordinator, courier, 'base' and money launderer are in many cases not clear cut in practice and quite often one person takes various roles. Small operations can work with only a coordinator, a courier and a person receiving the drugs abroad. Joe Brown Akubueze seemed to have been one of the major sponsors, the coordinator and the recipient of the drugs in 1993.

Managing risk is a key concern for drug traffickers, as the potential detection by law enforcement is the major threat they face.[46] One common way African smuggling networks spread the risk of detection by law enforcement is to send several couriers on the same flight – a practice called 'shotgunning' among law enforcers. While one courier might be arrested or even intentionally sacrificed by the network, the other couriers will have a greater chance to pass through as law enforcement is distracted. Risk is also decreased by strengthening cohesion and trust among network members, so that no network member is tempted to tip off the authorities or run away with the drugs. Trust between the different network members can be improved by involving only family members or friends in the core of the operation. Other actors are bound to the group through financial dependence or the need to return favours. Oaths or praying together also play a role in trust building, although some interviewed smugglers said that they avoid such practices as they can show weaknesses and attract law enforcement attention.

Most importantly, the available data and also the case of Joe Brown Akubueze show that smuggling is often conducted in the context of already established legal exporting and importing enterprises, for instance as part of a textile or car parts importing business. This integration into legal trading patterns also decreases the risk of law enforcement detection, although this is not usually a planned cover-up strategy, as argued by law enforcers, but almost a necessary precondition to enter the trade. Smugglers such as Joe Brown Akubueze need to have the experience of an import/export entrepreneur to be able and willing to join the trade in heroin and cocaine. In many cases, drug smuggling is simply a means of economic diversification for these entrepreneurs.

Slightly less is known about the third kind of drug smuggling in Mazzitelli's typology, which has seen large-scale consignments shipped through West African ports or waters since about 2005. This 'new bulk trade' has been different from the majority of local trafficking, not only because of the larger volumes of transhipped drugs, in particular cocaine, but also because of some new means of transport used, such as private aeroplanes and yachts. The majority of the recently detected large-scale shipments have nonetheless used containers. Most of these smuggling operations are also led by foreign individuals, in particular from Latin America and Europe, and West African members of these operations usually play a supportive rather than leading role.[47] For instance, in October 2011 a Gambian court found a group of Dutch, Venezuelan, Mexican and Nigerian smugglers guilty of trafficking more than 2 tonnes of cocaine into the country and hiding it in a fishing village. The operation was said to be directed by the European and Latin American network members.[48]

As these types of smuggling operations remain foreign-led and often just travel through West Africa's territory or waters, it is unclear how permanent and rooted this smuggling is in West Africa and whether law enforcers are merely seeing the most recent rerouting attempts of South American and European traffickers. Pessimistic views prevalent in international expert circles, however, have perceived the recent large-scale seizures as the first step of Africa's greater involvement in the cocaine trade.[49] These views also point to the favourable climate of impunity that weak and corrupt African states offer foreign smugglers, an argument that will be discussed in more detail in Chapter 4.

According to a few even more alarmist government reports, African drug smuggling networks have seen a further change more recently, as they have diversified into other illegal trades and graduated into mafia-like 'poly-crime organizations'.[50] It has been argued that African criminal networks have begun to not only smuggle drugs but a variety of other illegal commodities, and they have been involved in criminal activities, such as human trafficking and advance-fee fraud. There have even been reports about links between West African drug trafficking rings and terrorist groups linked to al-Qaeda.[51] While the available law enforcement data show that contacts between drug smugglers and criminals working in other fields have remained a rarity – the South African barter trade in illegal abalone and drug precursor chemicals mentioned in Chapter 1 being one important exception – it is doubtful if African drug smugglers are well qualified to engage in these other types of crimes, as the smuggling of drugs requires very different skills compared to sending out scam messages per email. The clearest evidence of links between drug smuggling and other criminal activities exists when smugglers purchase fake passports or bribe law enforcement officials, criminal practices hardly comparable to terrorism or human trafficking. Based on statements made by arrested smugglers, Africa's drug trafficking money is also not usually reinvested into other criminal activities but stays in the drug business or most frequently goes into other more socially acceptable trades. This pattern is made obvious, as many traders in illegal drugs also trade in legal goods, as was the case with Joe Brown Akubueze. Essentially, there are few documented, systematic links between drug smuggling and other serious criminal activities.

In this context, it also important to mention the relative lack of violence in much of Africa's drug smuggling. In portrayals instilled with the sensationalist war on drugs rhetoric, there have been many references to the brutality and 'cut-throat' nature of the heroin and cocaine traffic in Africa, comparing it to the Colombian and Mexican experience.[52] However, most of Africa's drug smuggling networks interestingly work without resorting to physical violence as an alternative means of contract enforcement or business competition. The reasons why African drug smuggling is less violent than in Colombia or Mexico are not well understood, but we can speculate that there are two major factors: the small-scale nature of the smuggling, and the lack of involvement in the more violent retail markets for heroin and cocaine, with the important exception of Nigerian involvement in South Africa's retail market where violence has been more common. African smugglers' role in the drug trade, however, usually stops with the wholesale of the drugs in the West, and very rarely are the drugs sold to street dealers or actual consumers.[53]

In general, due to the limited data available, there is a real danger of stereotyping and generalizing about 'African drug smugglers'. Some media reports and official statements inspired by the global drug war have given the impression that 'Africa's drug barons' hold immense powers and every poor African is tempted to smuggle drugs.[54] This is not the case. The great majority of Africans are not involved and are likely not to benefit from this trade at all. As was illustrated above, a few entrepreneurs diversify into the profitable but risky smuggling of heroin and cocaine and they do not recruit couriers from the poorest sections of Africa's societies such as the rural poor, but instead there is a clear preference for middle-aged, relatively educated individuals living in urban centres, who are struggling in the difficult economic circumstances existing in many African cities today.

A future Colombia?

Predicting the future of Africa's role in the global trade in drugs seems futile, as far too little is still known about the current extent of the drug trade in Africa. However, a look ahead based on recently gathered information is possible in so far as potential future scenarios for Africa's role in the drug trade can be described. The large-scale seizures of cocaine and heroin in the last few years show the persistent growth of the trade in these drugs through Africa, as well as Africa's consolidated role as a major global *entrepôt* for drugs. The regular detection of container shipments of drugs crossing the continent, continuously high numbers of African couriers arrested abroad, as well as the growing arrests of smugglers from major producing and consuming countries in Africa in the last few years are the strongest evidence that Africa is today an integral part of the global trade in heroin and cocaine and will remain so in the foreseeable future. UN officials even predict that these drugs are so important to African trade that it will not take too long before coca and opium are cultivated in African countries.[55]

Some of the recent concern and large-scale seizures across the continent are obviously a consequence of greater law enforcement vigilance in the past few years. As argued above, African countries already played an important role in the transit trade before the turn of the twenty-first century. Its role was just not as much on the radar of law enforcers and as extensively discussed by international policymakers as in the last decade. As a result of the global drug war's recent rediscovery of the continent, more African countries have become aware that cocaine and heroin are traded through their territories and waters and have made stronger efforts to detect drugs. In the short term, the still growing attention to the African drug trade in international policy, law enforcement and media circles is destined to produce some more large-scale seizures of cocaine but also heroin in the region. Due to the increased law enforcement focus on specific countries, such as Guinea-Bissau, new alternative transit hubs in the region or elsewhere in Africa might appear and it is possible that some existing hubs for cocaine have not yet been discovered by law enforcement, as the enforcers are always a few steps behind drug smugglers.

While much of what has been said about current and future trends in the African drug trade is speculative, it is clear that involvement in the transit trade – either in an entrepreneurial capacity or even as a courier – is an economically worthwhile and profitable endeavour for some Africans. Based on the little first-hand evidence available, drug smugglers in Africa evidently perceive the risks of interdiction and arrest, as well as the social stigma attached to trading an illegal substance, as worthwhile. Law enforcement efforts to stem the trade in Africa or abroad have had little effect on this perception as the routes and methods of smugglers simply adapt to new enforcement initiatives. In line with attempts to stop or contain the smuggling of drugs in other parts of the world, it is expected that the war on drugs will remain ineffective at influencing the African trade.[56] As experience in Latin American countries has shown, the focus on cocaine production and trade in one region has simply led to the dislocation of the trade to other regions and countries.

In fact, a dislocation of the drug trade away from its current main stage of West Africa to elsewhere on the continent or to somewhere outside Africa would be a modest best-case scenario. This would assume that African and international law enforcement efforts are effective enough to initiate such a shift in the trade. Many international experts are right to doubt the effectiveness of law enforcement efforts, as African states are not well equipped to halt the trade through their porous borders, and because there are few success stories of such a supply control-oriented policy elsewhere in the world, a debate that will be further explored in the next chapter.[57] In a more likely worse-case scenario, the transit trade would become further consolidated and domestic consumption, for instance of crack cocaine, would increase due to

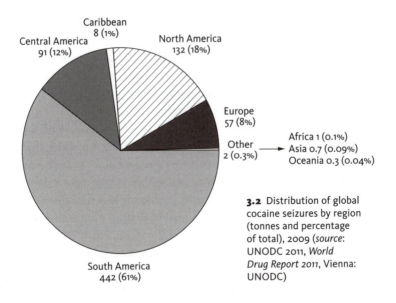

3.2 Distribution of global cocaine seizures by region (tonnes and percentage of total), 2009 (*source*: UNODC 2011, *World Drug Report 2011*, Vienna: UNODC)

a spillover from the expanding transit trade through Africa, leading to ever more repressive and foreign-inspired policy responses.

Nevertheless, there are some underlying reasons why African countries will never reach the level of involvement in the international heroin and cocaine trade as countries such as Colombia, Mexico or the US. One major difference between Latin American and African heroin and cocaine smuggling has been the volume of smuggled drugs. Quantities smuggled by African smugglers are still minor compared to large Latin American amounts shipped to the global centres of consumption. African smugglers carry comparatively small amounts by plane, and even though the number of couriers is high, the aggregate volume of heroin and cocaine smuggled is still small. Figure 3.2 provides an illustration of the African role in the cocaine market based on seizures. In 2009 the whole continent accounted for merely 0.1 per cent of global seizures. Only since 2005 have there been some reports of larger quantities smuggled through West Africa and of persistent increases. Although most of the 'new bulk trade' through West Africa is still coordinated by foreign drug entrepreneurs, this

Africa as entrepôt

might be an early indication of change in the drugs trade through the region.[58]

In essence, the African role in the international trade in heroin and cocaine is different from Latin American and western states because African countries are neither major producer nor consumer centres. Significant consumption of these drugs seems to be restricted to some urban centres in South Africa and the east coast at the moment and there have been no signs that opium and coca are making a comeback as agricultural cash crops on the continent. Long-distance smuggling is the main role of African actors and this means their position is less permanent in the international drug market compared to drug production and consumption centres. A smuggling industry can easily be shifted from one place to another due to changing interdiction patterns, but cultivation and consumption of drugs cannot.

In opium and coca producer countries, drug production generates numerous economic livelihoods and is more permanent. Compared to the few organizers and couriers of illegal drug smuggling, drug production involves a greater number of individuals, such as farmers, manufacturers and traders. In addition, the cultivation of drugs is less flexible, as plants cannot be uprooted and replanted at any moment. Therefore, the cultivation and preparation of opium and coca products are more fixed in place than the smuggling of the drugs.

But above all, consumer countries remain the most important and permanent centres of the trade in illegal drugs. Emmanuel Akyeampong has rightly argued that the focus on the criminal aspects of drug smuggling leads to a neglecting of the unchanged demand for illegal drugs in western consumer countries.[59] International demand for illegal drugs has been the driving force behind the evolution of large production centres, transit routes and hubs. Whereas the nationalities of smugglers and producers of illegal drugs have changed since the beginning of international drug control, the nationalities of the main consumers have not. Thus, Africa's role in the international trade in heroin and cocaine has been substitutable. The discourse of the global drug war, which has successfully labelled Africa as a global hub for the trade in heroin and cocaine, essentially sidelines the centrality of main consumer countries. The next chapter will examine how the global drug war has also manifested itself through drug control policies across the continent.

4 | African states and drugs: complicity, neglect and repression

Drug money is not only buying real estate and flashy cars: it is buying power. (Antonio Maria Costa, executive director, UNODC)[1]

In the last few years, West African states began to wake up to the dangers of the drug trade, which is swamping their tiny economies and corrupting – or further corrupting – their politics. (*New York Times*, 11 April 2010)[2]

The African state has been at the forefront of promoting drug control and at the same time it stands accused of being a major accomplice in the spread of the drug trade, as it is seen as either too weak to tackle the onslaught of traffickers or already actively involved in the illegal trade. This chapter examines both the role of the state as the major force against the trade of illegal drugs such as heroin, cocaine and cannabis, as well as African states' participation in this trade, showing that the international drug war rhetoric to 'strengthen weak African states' against the 'onslaught of illegal drugs' has had seriously negative consequences. While international pressures have led to increases of drug seizures and arrests on the continent, they have also tended to support highly draconian and ineffective drug policies and sidelined alternative approaches that stress the research, health and socio-economic dimensions of drug control. Furthermore, international policy-makers' focus on strengthening formal state actors, laws and their enforcement, has meant that the actual impact of these policies on the daily lives of Africans has remained ignored.

'Weak African states' and drugs

The role of the African state in the global drug trade has been debated since the early 1990s. Coinciding with the end of the cold war, a concern over the threat to global stability posed by weak, failed and collapsing African states became important in international policy debates. This policy concern was initially confined to states affected by civil wars, such as Sierra Leone and Somalia, but was later extended to a broader range of states, in particular the ones seen under threat from terrorist and criminal networks.[3] The growing importance of drug-related criminal activities in African countries since the late 1990s came to be seen as a consequence of state weakness in Africa and as the most obvious example for global criminal activities threatening stability in Africa and globally.

One of the earliest and most iconic portrayals of this threat came from Robert Kaplan in his highly influential *Atlantic Monthly* article in 1994 entitled 'The coming anarchy: How scarcity, crime, overpopulation, tribalism, and disease are rapidly destroying the social fabric of our planet'. This article became recommended reading for many officials in Washington and in European capitals and had a great impact on policy.[4] Emphasizing the global implications of developments in West Africa, Kaplan claimed:

> West Africa is becoming the symbol of worldwide demographic, environmental, and societal stress, in which criminal anarchy emerges as the real 'strategic' danger ... the increasing erosion of nation-states and international borders, and the empowerment of private armies, security firms, and international drug cartels are now most tellingly demonstrated through a West African prism.[5]

This concern about the regional and global implications of 'weak African states', 'state failure' and their links to international criminal activities has remained prevalent in policy circles until today, particularly among high-level US policymakers in the Department of Defense, who have been concerned about the opportunities that so-called 'ungoverned spaces' on the continent offer terrorists and criminals.[6]

There have always been two relatively distinct views about the role of African states in illegal activities. One view has seen

African states as institutionally too weak to deter drug traffickers and criminals. This 'weakness' has been illustrated most often through African states' porous borders and ineffective law enforcement. Due to a lack of resources and capacity, states are seen as necessarily neglectful of the drugs crossing their borders. Phil Williams argues that along with widespread poverty, urbanization and youth unemployment, a 'weak African state' and 'the lack of adequate forces dedicated to counternarcotics' contribute to the expansion of drug trafficking across the continent.[7]

The economist Francisco Thoumi in his seminal work on the spread of the cocaine industry in Colombia has made a related argument. He contends that the weak Colombian state gave the country a competitive advantage in the trade in illegal drugs, as the state was fragmented regionally and along party lines for a long time and the political centre lacked legitimacy among the majority of its population and hence it was not able to impose its norms on its population and counter the emerging cocaine trade. In slight contrast to Williams, Thoumi argues that poverty was not a significant factor in the Colombian case, as the country was wealthier than its Andean neighbours.[8] From the Colombian case it can be inferred that a context of economic underdevelopment and administrative weakness does not by itself lead to a country's attractiveness to illegal activities, as many states are 'poor' and 'weak' but few play a significant role in the drug trade. Thoumi points to a more underlying lack of state legitimacy that is significant, as well as the consideration of the historical circumstances of each state concerned. A comparable argument will be made in the case of African states and drugs.

A second more radical view has seen the African state not only as too weak in terms of enforcement capacity and legitimacy but increasingly as an accomplice in criminal activities. Such a view has become widespread among policymakers and in the media, as illustrated by the quotes at the outset of this chapter. The African state is described as being bought by powerful drug cartels, which gain official protection for their business or in even more extreme cases co-opt state actors into active positions within the trade.

William Reno and Jean-François Bayart have put forward the two most far-reaching accounts of the African state's complicit role in the drug trade. Drawing on the 1990s evidence from Liberia, Sierra Leone, Congo and Nigeria, Reno argues that in these states politicians and high-level officials actively seek involvement in commercial activities – many of them illegal – as a means to hold on to power. The context for this state transformation is the end of the cold war, which led to decreasing levels of international aid and foreign political support for African leaders and their domestic patronage systems. Without these resources, new illegal incomes have become integral for the rebuilding of political authority in African states.[9]

A related argument has been proposed by Bayart and associated researchers, who have claimed that African states and their economies are in the process of criminalization:

> Criminalization of politics and the state may be regarded as the routinization, at the very heart of political and governmental institutions and circuits, of practices whose criminal nature is patent.[10]

The reasons for this criminalization are similar to the ones suggested by Reno; the difference of this perspective is that Bayart takes the growth of drug trafficking through African countries and reports of high-level state involvement as key evidence of this trend.[11] Nigeria, Guinea-Bissau and Guinea-Conakry are mentioned as the prime examples of this drug-related criminalization.[12]

In the following, the chapter assesses the available evidence on 'state weakness' in the context of three different states. It will examine these countries' drug control policies and the evidence of active state involvement in the trade in drugs; and it will scrutinize the effects of the state's actions on the trade as well on its citizens more generally. The three countries examined are Guinea-Bissau, Lesotho and Nigeria. Two of the cases, Guinea-Bissau and Nigeria, are chosen because of the major role they play in public and academic debates on drugs and the state. While Guinea-Bissau and Nigeria's role will be discussed in the context of the heroin and cocaine trade, Lesotho is chosen for its major position in cannabis markets. There is an obvious difficulty in making generalizations about more than 50 diverse African states based on only three cases. Thus, the modest aim is to work out some common patterns of interaction between the state and drugs on the continent by drawing on three case studies of states. The three most common patterns are: state complicity in the trade; a state relatively neglectful of the trade; as well as a repressive state policy to control drugs.

The complicit state – Guinea-Bissau

Claims of state complicity in the illegal drug trade have been made in different African countries at different times. In the 1990s the Liberian pariah regime of Charles Taylor supposedly considered growing coca and cannabis as a means to undermine hostile western governments. In the late 1980s the Nigerian government and opposition figures regularly condemned each other for their involvement in the cocaine and heroin trade and more recently, the military regime of Captain Dadis Camara in Guinea-Conakry broadcast drug-related confessions of the former political elite on live television.[13] Recently published Wikileaks cables from US missions across the continent have suggested that even in internationally well-reputed governments in Nairobi, Freetown and Maputo, drug-related corruption is rife.[14] While it is unclear how credible the often politically inspired accusations have been, the unending line of scandals implicating political and diplomatic personalities in the drug trade indicate that elements of the state have clearly been complicit with drug traffickers. The best documented case of this pattern of high-level state involvement is Guinea-Bissau in the second half of the 2000s.

Guinea-Bissau, a small coastal state among the world's poorest and economically reliant on agricultural exports, has been labelled Africa's 'first narco-state' and portrayed as on the brink of falling into the hands of drug cartels. An influential International Crisis Group report of 2008 warned: 'There is real risk of [Guinea-Bissau] becoming a narco-state and a political and administrative no-man's-land, attractive to trafficking and terrorist networks in the Maghreb.'[15]

The same report also argued that 'state criminalization' is one of the most serious threats facing the country today. In a similar vein, the head of the UNODC argued in the preface to a report on Guinea-Bissau:

> The security implications for countries like Guinea Bissau go to the very core of the state's ability to maintain its sovereignty and integrity. There is a growing risk of some West African states being captured by foreign and local criminal networks colluding with senior officials, or even collapsing. While the situation is most acute in Guinea Bissau today, it could also develop somewhere else in the region tomorrow unless resolute steps are taken quickly.[16]

Aside from these official statements, reports in major international newspapers, such as the *New York Times*, *Sunday Times* and *Observer* of London, and Spanish *El País* have been equally important at influencing public discourse.[17] Many of these publications have depicted Guinea-Bissau as the 'world's first narcostate', in particular after the assassinations of the president and the head of the armed forces in March 2009, which were seen as a consequence of high-level struggles over the control of the cocaine trade. There have also been recurring claims that al-Qaeda, Hezbollah and the Colombian FARC had representatives in the country to profit from the flourishing drug trade and that they further instilled a climate of violence.[18]

Nonetheless, the political violence that international newspapers linked to the drug trade in 2009 has had a long history, as Guinea-Bissau faced several periods of political instability, coups and military rule, as well as a brutal war of independence in the 1970s and civil war in the late 1990s. To claim that much of this violence was due to drugs clearly simplifies the complex political history of Guinea-Bissau. Joshua Forrest has argued that much of this instability and violence – at times better termed state terror – was the consequence of a 'weak state' attempting to forcefully establish its control over its population and eliminate alternative power-holders. A history of underfunded Portuguese colonialism exacerbated the state's weakness and its inability to affect life outside the capital city. Importantly, Forrest is not arguing that the lack of state power has led to instability and violence, but that the state lacks legitimacy in the eyes of most Bissau-Guineans and has been the major initiator of violence and chaos in the late 1990s as well as in 2009. The illegitimate state in Bissau largely relied on coercion to exercise its power.[19]

The state has not only been weak and coercive in terms of extending its control over society, but has also been unable to enforce its control functions over its territory. This aspect of state weakness has been highlighted most often by international drug policymakers. The lack of passable roads, in particular during the rainy season, has been used as an obvious indicator of the weak administrative power. The country also has extensive unpatrolled land borders and a rugged coastline consisting of many small islands, which have made the detection of ships or planes carrying drugs even harder.

The country's criminal justice system has also seen major deficiencies. The most often cited problem has been the lack of prison facilities, which were only set up with the help of the UN in September 2010. International policy experts have reported how law enforcement lacks the most essential equipment, such as police cars to take suspected drug smugglers to the police station, and how law enforcers are easily corrupted because they are underpaid or not paid at all – a situation not uncommon in many other African law enforcement agencies.[20] Accordingly, Guinea-Bissau also had no drug control initiatives in place until the recent pressures from the UN and donor states.

These international pressures started to mount on the government in Bissau after the detection of large amounts of cocaine in the country, as mentioned in the preceding chapter. The largest seizures took place in September 2006 when 674 kilograms were detected in a raid on a private residence, in April 2007 when 635 kilograms were seized by police but an estimated 2.5 tonnes could not be confiscated due to lack of police capacity, and in July 2008 when a clandestine plane arriving from Venezuela landed and its suspected drugs cargo disappeared. In all three cases, significant amounts of the drugs disappeared and military officials either directly obstructed the work of the judicial police or were even seen removing drugs.[21]

Notwithstanding this strong evidence for military involvement in the drug trade, some of the subsequent claims about the state–crime nexus made in the media can be considered unfounded. There was no evidence for al-Qaeda, Hezbollah and FARC involvement in the drug trade. Two Mauritanian men with links to a North African terrorist group were indeed arrested by French police in Guinea-Bissau in December 2007; however, French officials confirmed that Guinea-Bissau was not a common hiding place for terrorists.[22] And according to most academic experts, the 2009 political assassinations were also not directly linked to the drug trade but a continuation of the bloody intra-elite conflict plaguing the country for decades.[23] Such unfounded claims about Guinea-Bissau's state complicity in the drug trade and its role in international terror networks should not only be considered as media sensationalism but also as attempts to galvanize donor attention. Some cynical observers have argued that Bissau-Guinean self-depictions as a 'narco-state' have been attempts to attract donor money, which has been much more sparse in Guinea-Bissau compared to other post-conflict countries, such as Sierra Leone and Côte d'Ivoire.[24]

Based on these claims and the large-scale seizures of cocaine, foreign donor interest undeniably increased in the second half of the 2000s. The UNODC and a wide range of other UN bodies and regional organizations, as well as donor agencies in particular from the European Union, have not only set the tone for the establishment of drug control but a broader 'security sector reform' since 2006. Whole state institutions, such as the police, military, judiciary and prisons are supposed to be restructured through these programmes. In the field of drug control, this has meant the establishment of new centralized drug units, various training programmes by foreign law enforcement agencies, such as the US DEA, as well as the provision of law enforcement equipment.[25] The focus has overwhelmingly been on 'strengthening the criminal justice system' and only some token – largely rhetorical – support has been offered to the growing crack cocaine-using population.

These technical assistance programmes of international organizations and donors already saw serious problems in the first few months of their work due to the volatile political situation in the country. An army mutiny in April 2010 leading to the replacement of top military officials necessitated the temporary suspension of much of the international donor funds and projects not only in the drug control field. The situation appeared highly dubious for most observers, as the coordinators of the mutiny had been on a US blacklist of major drug smugglers and at the same time had been under the protection of a UN office in Bissau in the run-up to the mutiny.[26] After a few months of showing their opposition to the unfolding events, the donors had no option but to gradually reaffirm their support for the government and continue their financial support for reform in the country, while the EU permanently suspended its security sector aid to the country.[27]

Considering its political and economic problems, drug control efforts have not been the highest priority in Guinea-Bissau until the recent international interventions. Many of the drug control initiatives established there in the second half of the 2000s have been driven by UN and donor interests, which largely meant improved interdiction of cocaine shipped through its ports. In any case, with the continued political instability facing the country, few long-term effects of these control policies can be expected. But as one Bissau-Guinean official stated, the political instability and high turnaround of government and military officials has made life much more difficult for drug smugglers, who need to find new supporters in government each time the leadership changes.[28] Ironically, political instability rather than the emerging drug control efforts of the state might be the best guarantee for the decline of Guinea-Bissau's status as a 'narco-state'.

This also shows that 'state weakness' and instability are not necessarily a beneficial condition for the drug trade to flourish. As already hinted at in the preceding chapter, more stable states, such as Kenya, Nigeria or South Africa, with their own share of corrupt officials and thriving ports, are much more attractive to traders in illegal as well as legal commodities. However, many of these states are also the key partners of the international donors and are unlikely to face too much pressure concerning their involvement in the drug trade.

The neglectful state – Lesotho

A second common pattern of interaction between African states and drugs is the deliberate neglect by the state, as well as a related strategy of farmers, traders and users successfully avoiding the state and its control policies. The popular strategy of avoidance has been a common pattern of state–society relations in African history until today, not merely in the inaccessible highlands of Lesotho.[29] Comparable examples can be found in Kenya's history of khat production during colonial times, where khat producers and traders successfully turned restrictive state regulation to their benefit or simply contested prohibition through the formation of a black market (see Chapter 2 for details).[30] A similar pattern is also common with the cultivation and trade in illegal cannabis across West Africa today. The state is often resented and easily avoided, in particular by farmers in rural areas. Cannabis is hidden among other crops, planted on land belonging to the state and larger cannabis farms are simply abandoned when police officers approach villages. In the southern African region, Lesotho is a telling story in this respect because of the significance of cannabis production to local communities and the national economy.

Lesotho is comparable to Guinea-Bissau in terms of its population and territorial size, although slightly more affluent according to such indicators as GDP or the Human Development Index.[31] This small mountainous and agriculture-based country, surrounded by the economically powerful neighbour of South Africa, has also had its periods of political instability, such as intra-elite violence in the late 1990s, although it has seen much less violence than Guinea-Bissau or its immediate neighbour South Africa with its own history of Apartheid and oppressive white minority rule. Despite its size, Lesotho is one of the world's major cannabis producers and a major supplier to the South African market. As discussed in detail in Chapter 2, Lesotho's cannabis has become a key cash crop in recent years and the growth in the cannabis industry has especially increased after the decline of labour migration to South Africa's mines and due to structural adjustment policies.

There is no question that cannabis production and trade have flourished because Lesotho is an administratively 'weak state'. Many of the mountain kingdom's villages are impenetrable to state officials and policy, not merely during times of the rainy season, when roads are impassable.[32] There are also obvious examples of state complicity in the flourishing cannabis trade, as police officers frequently receive bribes from drug smugglers at roadblocks and some local government officials have been reported to grow cannabis themselves. While such instances of state complicity have been on a low level and rarely involved high-level state officials, Lesotho's police and state authorities have often intentionally turned a blind eye to the cannabis trade and have even acknowledged this in interviews.[33] Law enforcers have seen no interest in dismantling a flourishing economic activity, particularly as it has secured many rural people's livelihoods. Thus, the state has intentionally neglected the enforcement of cannabis's illegal status.

The state has also lacked the capacity to enforce the illegality of the drug, as famers and traders have easily avoided the state altogether. Cannabis, or *matekoane* as it is locally known, is typically grown in isolated and not easily accessible parts of the mountains. Some of the local chiefs and strongmen have their own cannabis fields and have helped to shield the villagers from state attempts to identify the farms or have helped to pay off officers reaching the village. The state in these villages is essentially a policeman or a low-level government official paying the village an occasional visit. When such strangers approach, the farmers will leave their cannabis farms and hide until the strangers are gone. Hence, during the rare occasions of local state officials entering the mountainous villages, the state is simply avoided. Julian Bloomer argues that:

> [w]hile the community in Botsoapa [the village where Bloomer conducted his research] was largely positive about the involvement of NGOs in the village, there was a reluctance to engage with government agencies, especially when matters involving improved infrastructure, such as roads, have been proposed. The feeling in the community, as expressed by the sub-chief in Ha Mantsi during an interview, is that improved roads would also mean an end to the cannabis trade, 'You know *matekoane* is good but it still has a problem ... people think that it's not wise having roads because it will bring the police closer to them.' ... Improved roads would allow easier access for vehicles, especially the police, and enable the government to more effectively monitor areas where cannabis is grown.[34]

Thus, state policies, be they cannabis control or infrastructure projects, have often been opposed by villagers. This might seem irrational to an external observer but makes sense when the importance of cannabis to local livelihoods is considered. James Ferguson in his seminal study on development agencies in Lesotho has made a related argument when he showed how many villagers resented state initiatives of 'development', as such policies have often just been perceived as a means for the extension of the bureaucratic state apparatus into the lives of villagers.[35] They had little to do with the improvement of people's lives. Seen from this perspective, villages dependent on the cannabis trade have had strong incentives to avoid the state altogether, although it could be argued that their incomes still derived from the state's prohibition of the drug, which made the drug such a profitable commodity in the first place.

The state's neglect of the cannabis trade in Lesotho is also partly an outcome of international indifference to the country and its drug problems. While cannabis has played a critical role in

Lesotho's economy and its economic relations with South Africa, the drug has rarely been problematized in international policy discourse, as has been the case with cocaine in Guinea-Bissau. International policy experts have made no strong claims about drugs in Lesotho yet. For instance, in the UN's *Cannabis in Africa* report there are passing mentions of Lesotho's production and exports to South Africa, but the report remains silent on the domestic and regional significance of this trade as well as the state's possible role in it.[36]

The INCB sent a rare mission to the country in 2005 assessing the country's drug problems and drug control efforts. The mission was headed by the long-time Nigerian president of the INCB, Philip Emafo, and provided mainly praise for the country's drug supply and demand reduction initiatives – much of the national legislation was redrafted only a few months before the mission landed in Maseru. It found particular praise for the cannabis eradication and anti-trafficking efforts of the government and recommended better coordination and centralization of drug control efforts through the setting up of a national narcotics board for drug control. In addition to praise and recommended centralization, the mission also suggested alternative development initiatives to substitute the planting of cannabis with other legal crops. Interestingly, the same report featured a special section on the experiences of alternative development in other regions of the world – many of which were seen as not very successful and underfunded.[37] Nothing was heard of alternative development in the years after the INCB mission left the country, despite African governments' efforts to place cannabis crop substitution programmes on the international policy agenda. The only important impact of the mission seems to have been a large joint seizure of cannabis by Lesotho's and South Africa's police forces in 2006, which received further INCB praise.

It is also noteworthy that the cannabis trade in Lesotho has not been made a security issue in international policy circles, as has been the case with cocaine in West Africa. There have been no speculations about the cannabis trade's links to terrorism or its potential threat to regional and international security. It can be argued that this international indifference towards Lesotho's thriving cannabis production and the state's negligence has been due to the fact that Lesotho's cannabis is not as high up on the international policy agenda as is cocaine directly shipped to the European market. The drug war rhetoric has not yet fully integrated Lesotho and has allowed for its policy of neglect to continue to exist.

This international indifference to Lesotho's cannabis economy is not always shared by the country's powerful neighbour South Africa though. In recent years, there has been a flurry of South African media reports about the dangers of the influx of Lesotho's cannabis into the South African economy and possible links to other crimes, such as car theft and weapons smuggling. After the two governments signed an agreement on border control in June 2007, easing the movement of people across the borders, the growth of cannabis smuggling has been lamented by South African farmers in the adjacent province as well as by law enforcers.[38] In December 2009 the South African police chief called Lesotho a 'hotspot' for regional drug trafficking after large-scale seizures of cannabis had been made on the South African side of the border in the preceding months.[39] While this concern about the influx of cannabis from Lesotho has not yet reached the highest political level in Pretoria, this might change in the near future, especially considering the importance that crime plays in South African public discourse and the much greater willingness to adopt the global discourse on the war on drugs.[40]

As has been pointed out before, in Lesotho itself cannabis remains 'de facto decriminalized' today and it is only treated as a dangerous substance when it crosses the border into South Africa, although even the South African police have been unable and unwilling to 'crack down' on cannabis production on their own territory.[41] The only possible changes to this policy of open state neglect would come from South African and international pressures. However, considering the domestic reluctance to make cannabis a policy issue and the possibilities for popular opposition to such as state project, it is unlikely that changes to cannabis production in Lesotho would ever come from strengthened drug control efforts.

To reflect on what has been said, the Lesotho case shows how governments in Africa remain reluctant to interfere in the trade in drugs, as they are either not capable of enforcing prohibitions on the production, trade and use of drugs or they simply are not interested in making drugs an issue, especially if these drugs provide parts of their societies with important incomes. While this 'neglect' can be interpreted as relatively benign in the case of Lesotho and in other instances where drugs generate important livelihoods on the continent, state apathy can be detrimental when it concerns those that need help from the state, for instance drug users requiring medical treatment. This area of drug control has been ignored by states across the continent, as the following section will show.

The repressive state – Nigeria

When African states have shown a willingness to seriously implement policies to control the cultivation, trade and consumption of illegal drugs, these state responses have generally been repressive. Repression here means a police or military-driven policy to contain the production, trade and use of drugs by force, which usually comes at the cost of people's human rights. These state drug control campaigns often prioritize urban areas where law enforcement forces have enough resources to exert their power, although in some more resourceful states, such as South Africa and to some extent Nigeria, these campaigns have been extended to the countryside. Noteworthy examples are General Abacha's drug war in 1990s Nigeria, and Camara's more recent anti-drug campaigns in Guinea-Conakry. However, the tendency to implement harsh drug policies is also prevalent in more democratic states, such as Ghana, Kenya, Sierra Leone and today's Nigeria. Nigeria has not only had a long history of involvement in the drug trade but also extensive experience with drug control and therefore offers an important source for understanding the nature of state drug policy in Africa.[42]

As Africa's most populous and one of its strategically most important states, Nigeria is clearly different from the small states of Guinea-Bissau and Lesotho. The Nigerian state has had much greater administrative power, if one simply considers its extensive paved road network, and it has generally had more money to spend due to the large revenues from the export of oil – even if most of it is spent inefficiently and ends up in the pockets of the small elite. As one of the continent's major trading nations, its main port of Lagos has been an important staging post for the international drug trade since the 1980s.

Similar to Guinea-Bissau, the Nigerian state has faced periods of political instability and violent conflict in its history, with a brutal civil war in the 1960s and insurrections in the Niger Delta only being the most well known. Claims about Nigeria's potential disintegration into smaller parts have always been a common feature of popular and official discourse.[43] Violent conflict has often been seen as a reaction to the artificial nature of the state imposed through colonialism, but more frequently it was the state and intra-elite conflicts over its control that triggered or exacerbated instability and violence, as in the case of Guinea-Bissau. Long periods of military rule and highly coercive state policies from the 1960s onwards have also meant a further delegitimization of the state.[44] Thus, while the Nigerian state had more extensive resources at its disposal, it was at least as weak in terms of legitimacy as the other two states considered.

As in Guinea-Bissau and Lesotho, the Nigerian state has been both complicit in and neglectful of the drug trade. Most spectacularly, there have been claims about presidents being involved in the drug trade, for instance General Babangida and his wife were supposed to have benefited from drug smuggling activities in the 1980s. Nonetheless, such claims can largely be considered as rumours as Babangida and other members of the elite have clearly derived more significant incomes from the illegal diversion of oil revenues rather than the relatively small and stigmatized trade in heroin and cocaine. Yet there have been recurring scandals at the country's main drug agency and there is clear evidence of law enforcers' complicity in illegal activities, in particular in the early 1990s but also in the late 2000s. In 2010 Nigeria's drug tsar was sentenced to a lengthy prison term due to the protection offered to drug traffickers.[45] In addition to widespread drug-related corruption at the lower to mid-levels, authorities have also been successfully avoided by drug traders, farmers and users. This is most apparent with the rural cultivation of cannabis but is similarly the case with the urban distribution and use of cannabis and cocaine. In densely populated urban areas, such as Lagos Island, the sale and consumption of cannabis and crack cocaine is conducted quite openly and with the knowledge of local police officials.[46]

While complicity and state neglect are two common features to be observed, most Nigerians have perceived the state as a repressive actor. Nigerian drug control policy since the 1980s has been concerned with supply control and been implemented by law enforcement outfits with a reputation for corruption, brutality and extra-judicial killings. Violent and indiscriminate eradication campaigns to destroy farmland – at times killing farmers – illegal arrests and detentions, the frequent request of bribes at road checkpoints as well as the harassment of travellers at airports is the day-to-day face of drug control to many Nigerians. The peaks of these brutal campaigns occurred during the Buhari regime in the 1980s, when drug smugglers were publicly executed, as well as under Abacha in the 1990s, when there began cannabis eradication and campaigns to indiscriminately seize property of Lagos traders reputed to smuggle drugs. In the 1990s, Nigeria's drug agents were also well known for illegally extorting money from Nigerians through a policy of 'arrest to loot'. Axel Klein recounts the story of an ex-soldier who was imprisoned for smoking cannabis and who not only lost his freedom but also his assets to the drug agents:

The NDLEA [Nigeria's drug agency] came to my house one night. They had been informed by my neighbour that I was smoking hemp. I have been smoking for 22 years and have never been in any trouble. They break into my house and carried off all my property, the TV, videos, my papers, my pension.[47]

Although the rhetoric of the drug war has been slightly moderated since the end of the Abacha regime in 1998, many of the draconian and human rights-violating policies introduced under Buhari and Abacha have become institutionalized and continue in their original form until today. Drug control and money laundering laws established under the military have largely survived unamended. As in the 1990s, they give the authorities excessive powers to arrest, seize assets of suspects and publicly parade them before they have their trial. There is also clear evidence that drug-related suspects are ill-treated and tortured in detention cells and in overcrowded Nigerian prisons while they are 'awaiting trial' for months and sometimes for years.[48] While international drug policymakers have been impressed by the high number of arrests and convictions (usually of small-scale cannabis users, farmers and smugglers) as well as successful extraditions of drug traffickers (many of them not following due process of Nigerian law), this is the rarely mentioned, repressive reality of drug law enforcement for most Nigerians.

Aside from the harsh nature of state drug control, the exclusion of alternative views and the stifling of a public debate about drugs has been another dimension of Nigeria's drug war. In 1989 Nigeria established a centralized agency to conduct all matters related to drug control – even though this agency has only seriously attempted to fulfil its border interdiction and cannabis eradication mandate. In the course of the 1990s the National Drug Law Enforcement Agency (NDLEA) gradually sidelined alternative actors in the drug control framework, such as the Ministry of Health, and more importantly the NDLEA's central role has meant that alternative voices on drug control from the medical, NGO and academic world have been excluded from policymaking altogether. In fact, the establishment of the drug agency, as well as the repressive military regimes of Babangida and Abacha, helped to systematically marginalize Nigerian medical, academic and other experts on drugs that had engaged in a relatively open debate about the direction of the country's drug control approach in the second half of the 1980s. At the time these debates were even reproduced in the national media and included whole editorials dedicated to drugs and drug policy in the country. Little of this debate was left by the mid-1990s, at the heyday of Abacha's regime. The few surviving alternative views, for instance doctors concerned with the treatment of problematic drug users, have become very critical of state policy but also largely excluded from policymaking. They see the country's drug control system as 'totally skewed towards the judiciary, law enforcement system and the intelligence service' and putting foreign over domestic interests. The NDLEA has been heavily criticized for overlooking the crucial area of treatment and rehabilitation and instead is said to have made a Nigerian drug user in need of therapeutic help a criminal.[49] It is telling that other West African states, such as Sierra Leone, are now following into the footsteps of Nigeria's NDLEA by setting up similar centralized and exclusive agencies and drug control structures that are likely to stymie any debate about drugs and drug control.[50]

Nigeria's drug war has long been supported by international drug agencies. Since the mid-1980s Nigeria has worked closely with the US DEA and UN drug bodies. Nigeria was the first country in Sub-Saharan Africa with permanent US and UN drug representatives dedicated to assisting Nigerian policymakers. This was particularly important in the 1980s, when the Nigerian drug agency was modelled on its US counterpart. Since then the volume of foreign drug control aid and operational cooperation between US and Nigerian law enforcers has expanded immensely and the country has been praised widely for its war on drugs, without taking into account the human rights-violating nature of Nigerian drug control. US Assistant Secretary of State for African Affairs Johnnie Carson has been just one of many international supporters of Nigeria's drug war:

> Despite the significant challenges facing West Africa, there is reason for hope. Oil-wealthy Nigeria is entirely unique: numerous and very experienced Nigerian traffickers have been deployed worldwide over decades. But despite its many problems the Government of Nigeria has demonstrated increased

political will in fighting narcotics. US-donated body scanners at Nigeria's four international airports are having a deterrent effect, causing traffickers to shift their operations to seaports and land borders, where adequate protection is lacking, or to airports in neighboring countries. Nigeria's National Drug and Law Enforcement Agency (NDLEA) flexed its muscles in arresting a drug kingpin, processing an extradition, and convicting 1,231 of 1,239 traffickers in 2008. The Attorney-General recently approved the embedding of a USG [US government] sponsored drug investigations specialist within the NDLEA.[51]

It is no wonder that this close cooperation with international agencies has earned Nigeria much praise and the country has come to be seen as a model of African drug law enforcement in international policy circles since the early 2000s. In particular US drug agencies thought that Nigeria had 'assumed a leadership role in drug law enforcement in the region'.[52] Nigerians have started to train law enforcers from other countries at a UN-sponsored drug control academy and have coordinated West Africa-wide enforcement campaigns together with the US DEA. Nigeria has also been a driving force behind sub-regional drug policy initiatives, such as the Economic Community of West African States (ECOWAS) Plan of Action on Drug Control and the Round Table on Drugs and Crime in Africa, which was co-organized with the UN in Abuja in 2005.

However, the 'Nigerian success story' of drug control has continued to be heavily criticized, in particular by Nigeria's NGO and medical expert community. From these perspectives, the international praise has glossed over the draconian, human rights-violating approach taken by Nigerian authorities and the corrupt nature of Nigerian law enforcement and state. Most importantly, the critics have argued that the Nigerian drug war has had little to show in terms of successes, apart from seizures of drugs at airports. The drug trade through Lagos, which has existed since the 1970s, seems not to have been affected much by these efforts. Furthermore, the drug war has not only meant repression and lack of success, it has meant the embrace of non-evidence-based policy, as little research lies at its basis and it has also blatantly ignored the growing consumption of drugs in Lagos.[53]

In summary, the Nigerian case is not only important because the country has had a long history in the trade and control of drugs (arguably the longest on the continent); beyond this, Nigeria's drug war has started to serve as a model in international drug policy circles. A policy inspired by foreign ideas and clearly in line with the rhetoric of the global drug war is being replicated across the West African sub-region and beyond.

Implications of the global war on drugs

The stories of Guinea-Bissau, Lesotho and Nigeria draw attention to the major problems with official and academic portrayals inspired by the rhetoric of the drug war. First, many of these portrayals have made glib generalizations across the continent, by labelling African states as 'weak states' or 'narco-states'. In fact, the experiences of these three countries hint at the diversity of states and their individual histories of 'weaknesses' and also the varied roles they have played in the drug trade.[54] The importance of the patterns highlighted – complicity, neglect and repression – has changed over time in each individual case and has occurred in some states simultaneously. The experiences presented are by no means exhaustive of drug control in Africa. While West African states' drug control history can in many ways be compared to Nigeria's and there is an observable process of convergence of domestic policies, Ghana, for instance, has placed a slightly stronger emphasis on health-driven policies.[55] The same is true for Tanzania's recent experiments with harm reduction mentioned in Chapter 1, which are exceptional on the continent. Furthermore, South Africa with its industrialized base and historical experience of Apartheid has made it rather unique and difficult to associate with other states on the continent.

There is, however, a major commonality among all states discussed – even shared by South Africa – that has remained largely ignored in the rhetoric of international policymakers. The

African states and their drug policies mentioned have clearly lacked legitimacy in the eyes of most of their citizens. Most states have done so since colonial times, as their rule was often perceived as not based on any sufficiently accepted authority, but rather as coercive, corrupt and tools of elite enrichment. More importantly in the context of drug control, their policies were seen as impositions, mostly foreign, and executed primarily through the coercive arm of the government. The UNDCP's *Drug Nexus in Africa* report succinctly summarizes how such measures are seen by many in Africa:

> Local communities [in Africa] are unlikely to cooperate in drug control efforts when only negative penalties are perceived to be the consequence of cooperation. Public information in Africa has not succeeded in addressing the benefits that accrue from drug control cooperation. At present, the negative results – reduction in rural income, imprisonment of community members – are widely recognized by the communities whose involvement in drug control is nothing less than essential, but the positive results are not.[56]

While most official and academic claims about the danger of drugs to African states saw 'state weakness' as a key factor, few perceived this to be an underlying legitimacy problem. States in Africa, as well as their most apparent institutions such as the police or the military, are obviously a problem not only because they are not effective at stopping the drug trade or because some of them are involved in the trade, but because they and their policies are not credible in the eyes of their people. Thus, it is not surprising that these policies have faced difficulties of implementation, are often avoided and resisted, and remain largely ineffective.

A further problem with official portrayals was their view of the drug trade and the state's role in it as a technical issue, such as a lack of state capacity, porous borders, missing judicial or security sector reform or state failure. Based on such depictions, Africa's drug problems become well tailored to the mandates of international agencies dealing with drug and crime control; however, these depictions ignore the socio-economic and political complexities involved in policymaking domestically.[57] They see Africa's drug problems as isolated from the global drug market, in particular from the high demand for these substances in western countries. These views also ignore the realities of state power, the lack of legitimacy and intra-elite struggles over control of the state. The case of Guinea-Bissau is most revealing in this respect, as drug control policies sponsored by international donors are implemented in a highly volatile political situation, and while the donors are clinging to their notion of politically neutral technical assistance, they are inevitably pulled into domestic power struggles.

Moreover, the experience of African countries shows that international discourse on 'weak', 'failing' or 'narco-states' and policies to support these states have often meant a strengthening of the state's repressive capabilities and been at the expense of people's human rights. The technical assistance programmes to strengthen state capacity, border control and judicial reform have usually meant more weapons, cars and gadgets for police officers, more harassment by officials at borders and airports and longer sentences for the few small-scale drug criminals caught by the police. Such policies have simply meant an extension of the powers of state agencies, such as the police and military, disliked by many Africans, in particular where these institutions have been associated with colonial and postcolonial authoritarianism. This is where the rhetoric of the global war on drugs has had its most visible impact on African societies.

Over the last ten years, the UN, donors, African regional organizations and governments have aimed to go beyond simple policy rhetoric and have established a manifold of institutions to counter Africa's role in the drug trade. Some of these institutions have already been mentioned in the three country case studies above. Action plans by the African Union, ECOWAS and its equivalents in South and East Africa have set the agenda for the years to come. The major task is defined as stopping the growing supply of drugs from the continent. While a few of the lofty goals in the action plans mention the need for a better understanding of

Africa's drug problems and health-related concerns, the policies implemented based on such plans have prioritized the tougher interdiction, prosecution and punishment of drug criminals. An array of new institutions – many of them still only exist in name – has been set up by the UN and international donors, such as Transnational Crime Units (TCUs), West African Joint Operations, the West Africa Coast Initiative, the Dakar-based Inter-governmental Action Group Against Money Laundering, as well as their equivalents in South and East Africa. They all address the ability of domestic law enforcement agencies to better detect heroin and cocaine shipments and related problems of money laundering. Comparatively little money and effort has been spent on supporting underfunded African universities studying drugs and hospitals treating problem drug users.

The UN, in particular, has pinned its hopes to the establishment of new African law enforcement units, the TCU in policy discourse, in recent years:

> TCU will be elite inter-agency units, trained and equipped to fight transnational organized crime and to coordinate their activities in an international framework. This innovative concept could be expanded beyond the initial four target States to serve as a model for all ECOWAS members.[58]

The establishment of these TCUs is symbolic of the approaches promoted by international policymakers and implemented by their collaborators in African governments. They follow the Nigerian example of centralization of control and the exclusion of 'non-elite' policy views. They are directed at the interests of international donor countries, and these agencies are supposed to work very closely with the likes of the US DEA and other western law enforcement outfits. Above all, the TCU initiative clearly represents the prioritization of drug supply control over any alternatives concerned with drug user treatment or even most basic research on drug problems in Africa. Our concluding chapter will examine these possible alternatives – some of which have already been mentioned in this and in previous chapters.

Conclusion: alternatives to the drug war?

There is no drug policy, except for the interception of
drugs and this is a failing game ... They don't even know
the drug problem – their officers deny the Nigerian drug
problem. (Coordinator of a drug treatment NGO, Lagos)[1]

In our Introduction, we set out to answer a number of key questions related to drug production, trade, consumption and policy
in Africa. Over the course of four chapters, we have addressed
all but one of these questions. To recap:

*What is the historical depth to African drug production, trade,
consumption and policy?*

Drugs in Africa and their associated dangers have been presented as relatively new phenomena on the continent. However,
evidence points to a long history of drug consumption and trade,
from cannabis in fourteenth-century Ethiopia, to the centuries-
old practice of kola nut consumption and trade in West Africa
and khat in the East. The consumption of fermented beverages
is an ancient practice too. While much more recent, the history
of such substances as cocaine and heroin on the continent goes
back further than might be imagined: they have been consumed
for over 30 years and trafficked even longer in countries such as
Nigeria. Drug policy too has a significant history on the continent,
as, for example, the history of khat prohibition and control in East
Africa suggests. Attempts to control consumption no doubt have
an even longer history, as pre-colonial societies tried to restrict
consumption to those deemed able to consume responsibly. This
has led to some nostalgia for days when elders alone were able
to consume stimulants and intoxicants, and the concomitant
lament of current uncontrolled consumption by youth.

What is the extent of drug consumption in Africa? What substances are consumed in what socio-cultural settings? And how fearful should we be?

Drug use permeates all countries in Africa to some degree, though by far the most consumed substances are alcohol, tobacco and caffeinated beverages. There are great variations in how such substances are consumed, with much consumption diverging from western 'drug culture': cannabis, for example, is often consumed in functional rather than recreational contexts, and a number of substances are used medically and ceremonially. The use of 'harder' drugs such as heroin appears to converge more with western usage, and drug culture among the wealthy in South Africa resembles clearly the club culture prevalent in Europe and North America. In some regions, fashions for particular drugs have created worrying trends, including methamphetamine consumption in South Africa, and heroin consumption along the East African coast. Most consumers of such substances are youth, often from marginalized communities. While some substances such as khat are now integrated within a youth culture, youthful consumption is almost always a major source of concern about drugs. However, little evidence exists to suggest that drugs are the source of widespread harm for African youth, or that their problematic consumption is a cause of societal harm, rather than a symptom of wider social problems. Indeed, given the vast scale of their use, the powerful vested interests that promote their use, and their known association with medical and social harm, it is alcohol and tobacco – the legal drugs – that most likely pose the greatest threat to Africans.

How damaging to development are the production, trade and use of drugs in Africa?

Received wisdom dominates debate about drugs and their impact on Africa, and this is especially so in regard to discourse about drugs and development on the continent. Increasing drug production, trade and consumption is reckoned to be a major impediment to the fulfilment of the Millennium Development

131

Goals. Again, little evidence that drugs are a major impediment to African development exists, and drug policy itself, rather than the substances it seeks to control, can be seen as the root cause of many development harms such as increased corruption. Rather than being necessarily a harm to development, the production of two of Africa's major drug crops – cannabis and khat – have instead provided livelihoods for thousands of farmers, as well as traders and transporters along their commodity chains, helping sustain households, villages and whole districts at times of severe economic stress. Of course, relying on incomes from substances seen so negatively by international policymakers has its dangers; however, in most cases the benefits to famers have outweighed the risks. As we discussed at the end of Chapter 2, even the consumption of these substances is not necessarily anti-development either.

Will Africa's role as entrepôt *in the trade of heroin and cocaine further expand and lead to the emergence of 'narco-states'?*

Our look at Africa's incorporation into transnational flows of cocaine and heroin supply suggests that predictions of the continent's ever-growing global role in the trade and the formation of 'narco-states' in West Africa are exaggerated. Here again, we challenge ahistorical portrayals of Africa's role in the drug trade as well as the drug war rhetoric on African 'drug barons', 'cartels' and violent trafficking through an assessment of the emergence of and the actual actors in Africa's cocaine and heroin connection. While the trade in these two drugs has expanded over the last decade and is likely to grow in the next few years, despite international and African control efforts, the trade is not destined to grow unlimitedly. Africa is not a major consumer or producer of hard drugs, and the role of countries such as Guinea-Bissau as *entrepôts* is essentially substitutable, and likely to shift as established trafficking routes become known and policed, and hence less attractive. Some of the moral panic about 'narco-states' seems to have been encouraged by African governments themselves, as was shown in the case of Guinea-Bissau, in the quest for access to further policing resources and donor funds.

*How has the war on drugs manifested itself in different
African countries? And how have different states actualized
international drug policy?*

Drug policy is by no means uniform in Sub-Saharan Africa,
and different states have approached policy in a variety of ways.
We describe three different 'ideal types' of state policy towards
drugs: complicity, neglect and repression. Clearly, none of these
three ideal types offers a model for a future drug policy. While
we found that high-level state complicity is still a rarity and
official neglect of drug use, trade and cultivation much more
widespread, the most active application of drug policy has relied
on supply reduction strategies that are often at odds with human
rights and the supposed main purpose of drug control: to address
the risk to people from drug consumption. The dangers of drug
consumption are not countered, while arguably greater harm is
induced by repressive criminal justice measures.

We argue that the tone for the current policy discussions about
Africa's growing role in the drug trade has to some extent already
been determined by the rhetoric of the 'global war on drugs'
and by the laws and institutions set up over the last few years.
Law enforcement approaches have been prioritized in the history
of global drug policy as well as in recent efforts to strengthen
African drug control. With many of the policies and institutions
driven by foreign concerns, it comes as no surprise that African
official discourses on drugs have been shaped by western ideas
on drugs and their supply-sided control. If the war on drugs is
failing in Africa, as elsewhere in the world in the view of a growing movement of researchers and activists, including the IDPC
or the Count the Costs project, what are the alternatives? It is
now time to look at the final question posed in the Introduction.

*What room is there in Africa for alternative perspectives and
policies that diverge from the received wisdom of prohibition?*

Compared to policy deliberations in western states, there is
very little debate about alternative drug policies in Africa today. There are no discussions in professional or popular circles

about the benefits of more 'balanced' drug policy approaches, harm reduction and decriminalization as in the West, nor about 'home-grown' policy alternatives, for instance by drawing on the long continental history of regulating and taxing drugs, such as alcohol, khat and kola.[2] Discussions about these policies only exist on the very margins of national policymaking, which remains dominated by law enforcement agencies and their final aim of 'drug-free' African societies.

Even if sidelined, alternatives exist. The South African policy on drugs was already mentioned as rather exceptional in previous chapters. According to its drug control strategy, this African country adheres to a relatively 'balanced' drug control approach dedicating equal importance to drug interdiction, treatment, drug use prevention as well as harm reduction. In Western Cape Province this approach to drug control has been most seriously implemented as health professionals have driven policy implementation. However, in the rest of the country the 'balanced' approach in line with the international policy counter-currents mentioned in this book's Introduction, remains a policy statement without actual effect, as most money is spent on the South African police's repressive drug supply control rather than on potentially contentious issues such as needle exchanges for heroin users.[3] South Africa's 'balanced' approach largely exists on paper and hence the country's approach to drug control is not too different from that of the rest of Africa.

More importantly, harm reduction is currently discussed in expert circles in a few countries such as Tanzania, Mauritius and Kenya due to an acknowledged problem with injecting heroin use and HIV/AIDS. There have also been several foreign-led research initiatives and lobbying for the usefulness of measures such as needle exchange and methadone maintenance on the East African coast. Despite the extensive praise from international medical experts, it is still to be seen if the methadone programme experiment started in Dar es Salaam in February 2011 will survive pressures from drug war-inspired views that see it as promoting drug use rather than total abstinence.[4] Debates on the value of harm reduction as an alternative to draconian prohibitionist poli-cies are non-existent in most other African states, although these countries potentially face the same drug-related health problems as Tanzania.

There is even less of a debate about more contentious policy alternatives, such as decriminalization and legalization. Rwanda and South Africa have been exceptional in this respect of late, as a move towards decriminalizing cannabis has been propagated, especially by health officials in these countries.[5] While reform proposals in South Africa – some of these initiatives surprisingly originate within the state bureaucracy itself – are unlikely to make it on to the policy agenda dominated by the drug war rhetoric, in Rwanda such proposals reached the parliament in 2010. The proposed law drafted by the minister of health essentially aims to introduce cannabis as a painkiller in hospitals in the country as well as a non-toxic alternative to chemotherapy. This is not a revolutionary proposal legalizing the drug altogether and making it available more widely. In fact, cannabis has already been used illegally as a painkiller in several African countries, especially in southern Africa. If it passes into law, the Rwandese proposal will provide for a cheap pain-relieving option for doctors in certain hospitals. It will be similar to the morphine already administered in African hospitals despite shortages, and will be well within the international legal framework that permits the use of cannabis, opiates and cocaine for medical purposes. The proposal basically extends the health dimension of cannabis and decriminalizes some of its uses.

While there have not been more than a handful of these state-driven alternatives to the dominant law enforcement and supply-oriented drug control approach across the continent, some NGOs and religious groups have preached and practised differ-ent types of drug control. Most of these groups have prioritized the treatment of drug users, often with the most basic means possible. The Omari Project already mentioned is one of the few organizations that offer problem drug users, especially of heroin, a cheap, professional and relatively effective option of treatment on the Kenyan coast. It also offers researchers a rare but important glimpse into heroin use patterns in this part of Africa. In West and South Africa there is a range of similar NGOs, many of them with a religious orientation, such as the Lady of Victory Rehabilitation Centre in Jos in Nigeria run by a Catholic priest. This group mainly uses 'spiritual treatment' for its clients, which means they pray with cannabis, heroin and alcohol users.[6] It remains uncertain how successful such kinds of underfunded treatment can be with more serious problem drug users who would require medical attention. Research on Nigeria shows that for many problem users, however, these religious treatment centres are more likely places of relief than psychiatric state hospitals, as the latter charge large amounts of money for a treatment programme and few drug users are inclined to admit themselves to a psychiatric institution, as they do not want to be seen as having mental health problems.[7]

Other NGOs, such as the Centre for Research and Information on Substance Abuse (CRISA), which publishes the *African Journal on Drug and Alcohol Studies*, have concentrated on researching Africa's drug problems. Drugs and drug policy in Africa have largely been ignored by the international activist and reformist movement on drug control – the IDPC had until very recently no African members for instance – and CRISA is one of the few drug NGOs on the continent with strong links overseas. Its journal remains the continent's most important forum for the discussion of alternative policy approaches and several of its contributions, at times written by foreign experts, have dealt with contentious policy options, such as harm reduction and decriminalization. However, it is telling that much of this pan-African research has had little impact nationally, as governments have almost system-atically excluded the academic and health experts publishing in these journals.

The war on drugs discourse supported by international aid has been sidelining alternative views emanating from health sectors and academia. The most obvious example of this sidelining of alternatives was US drug-related aid during the George W. Bush administration, when any US initiatives with the slightest harm reduction component received no US funding. It is through such financial pressures, and also through more subtle rhetoric adaptations mentioned throughout this book, that the global drug war has sidelined changes to drug policy in Africa.

These alternative views might of course not always be less repressive than the supply control measures prioritized by African governments and international policymakers mentioned in Chapter 4. For instance, cannabis users are often coerced by doctors, priests and their families to go through treatment in hospitals and in other treatment centres in Africa. And even Portugal's recently reformed 'liberal' drug policy has its coercive elements, such as compulsory meetings of drug users with so-called 'dissuasion panels'.[8] Nonetheless, the key is not how liberal, non-prohibitionist and non-coercive these alternatives are but that there is a debate about drugs, drug policy and possible alternatives. This debate does not exist in most African countries.

This lack of a debate cannot simply be blamed on foreign drug policy interventions or a global war on drugs. Most African governments remain reluctant to acknowledge and investigate the impact of drugs on their societies and few question the implications of drug policies themselves. There is a clear lack of information on drug use in Africa, even on such worrying trends as injecting heroin use, as well as on the potentially lethal use of fake pharmaceutical drugs across the continent. In countries such as Nigeria and Senegal, the dangers of these 'legal' drugs have recently received much media attention, but little has been done to examine their spread and impact on people's health. While many governments have started to reinforce their anti-drug police forces, they are unwilling to provide funds for treatment of problematic heroin users and research on fake medicines.

In particular, drug users in need of medical support receive no help from the state. Sheryl McCurdy's work with heroin users in East Africa has shown that users are left fending for themselves or at times act together against a domestic and international environment that has stigmatized them as criminals and outcasts.

Female sex workers using heroin pool their incomes to rent a safe place to live and use drugs; and some more powerful women protect younger ones from the violence they face on a day-to-day basis in the city.[9] McCurdy suggests that supporting these initiatives of heroin users themselves would be a viable option for spending international aid.

A first step to move beyond repressive and ineffective state drug control in Africa would be to spark national debates on drugs, for instance in the media, thus promoting discussions of drug policies and their actual effects on African societies. These debates have existed in some countries – Nigeria in the 1980s and Tanzania more recently – but are stifled too soon by domestic and international drug war rhetoric. Now is the moment to provoke such debates across Africa, as international efforts to frame African drug problems have only just started in many countries, and it is vital that Africans, including those most affected by drugs – users, traders and farmers – play their role in shaping the debate. From this debate, policies for problematic drug use might emerge that are not beholden to the 'one size fits all' supply-side model that is being imposed on Africa at present; at the least, policymakers in Africa and beyond may learn much to help them more wisely allocate resources to programmes that make a real difference, for example, harm reduction measures such as needle provision to curb the spread of blood-borne diseases among injecting drug users.

As to the war on drugs itself, surely it is time for the international community to jettison an approach that has proved so ineffective at curbing the drugs trade and drug consumption, yet so effective in creating oppressive laws and profits for smugglers and in sidelining more humane approaches to the treatment of problem drug users. The war on drugs approach is not going to be any more successful in Africa than it has been elsewhere; indeed, in many ways Africa has more to fear from the uncritical application of such failed policy than it does from the drugs themselves.

Notes

Introduction

1 Statement reprinted in *BBC News*, 'Africa – new front in drugs war', 9 July 2007. Available at: http://news.bbc.co.uk/2/hi/africa/6274590.stm (accessed January 2012).

2 Statement reprinted in *Voice of America*, 'US Senate panel warns of increasing drug trafficking in West Africa', 23 June 2009. Available at: www.voanews.com/english/news/a-13-2009-06-23-voa56-68789137.html (accessed January 2012).

3 Richard Nixon statement to the press, 1972. Available as a YouTube clip: www.youtube.com/watch?v=bsrxpVUKUK0 (accessed December 2011).

4 James Mills (2007) 'Colonial Africa and the international politics of cannabis: Egypt, South Africa and the origins of global control', in James Mills and Patricia Barton (eds) *Drugs and Empires: Essays in Modern Imperialism and Intoxication, c.1500–c.1930*, Houndmills: Palgrave, pp. 165–72.

5 For an authoritative account of international drug control efforts, see William McAllister (2000) *Drug Diplomacy in the Twentieth Century: An International History*, London: Routledge.

6 ibid., pp. 230–6.

7 UNODC (2003) *Operational Priorities: Guidelines for the Medium-term*, Vienna: UNODC, pp. 3–4.

8 *BBC News*, 'Bolivia's Evo Morales says no to DEA agents' return', 4 March 2011. Available at:www.bbc.co.uk/news/world-latin-america-12643404 (accessed January 2012).

9 Robin Room (1999) 'The rhetoric of international drug control', *Substance Use & Misuse* 34 (12): 1700–01.

10 Caitlin Hughes and Alex Stevens (2007) 'The effects of decriminalization of drug use in Portugal', *Beckley Foundation Briefing Paper 14*. Available at: http://kar.kent.ac.uk/13325/1/BFDPP_BP_14_EffectsOfDecriminalisation_EN.pdf.pdf (accessed December 2011).

11 David Courtwright (2001) *Forces of Habit: Drugs and the Making of the Modern World*, Cambridge, MA: Harvard University Press, pp. 201–3.

12 See the following report posted by an organization called the Harm Reduction Coalition: www.harmreduction.org/article.php?id=999 (accessed December 2011).

13 For a description of the

139

internal UN debates on harm reduction, see David Bewley-Taylor (2005) 'Emerging policy contradictions between the United Nations drug control system and the core values of the United Nations', *International Journal of Drug Policy* 16: pp. 427–8; UN News Centre, 'Human rights, harm reduction key to drug policy, UN rights chief says', 10 March 2009. Available at: www.un.org/apps/news/story.asp?NewsID=30135&Cr=UNODC&Cr1= (accessed January 2012).

14 Jack Donnelly (1992) 'The United Nations and the global drug control regime', in Peter H. Smith (ed.) *Drug Policy in the Americas*, Boulder, CO: Westview Press.

15 ibid., p. 288.

16 Martin Jelsma (2003) 'Drugs in the UN system: The unwritten history of the 1998 United Nations General Assembly Special Session on Drugs', *International Journal of Drug Policy* 14 (2): 192.

17 www.idpc.net/ (accessed January 2012); www.countthecosts.org/ (accessed January 2012).

18 Cindy Fazey (2003) 'The Commission on Narcotic Drugs and the United Nations International Drug Control Programme: Politics, policies and prospect for change', *International Journal of Drug Policy* 14 (2): 156–7.

19 The most recent call came from a group of ex-presidents, economists and business people, among others: www.guardian.co.uk/world/2011/may/29/drugs-trade-drugs (accessed December 2011).

20 UNDCP (1999) *The Drug Nexus in Africa*, Vienna: UNDCP, p. 17.

21 Emmanuel Akyeampong (1996) *Drink, Power, and Cultural Change: A Social History of Alcohol in Ghana, c.1800 to Recent Times*, Oxford: James Currey; Jonathan Crush and Charles Ambler (1992) *Liquor and Labor in Southern Africa*, Athens: Ohio University Press; Justin Willis (2002) *Potent Brews: A Social History of Alcohol in East Africa, 1850–1999*, Oxford: James Currey.

22 Emmanuel Akyeampong (2005) 'Diaspora and drug trafficking in West Africa: A case study of Ghana', *African Affairs* 104 (416): 429–47; Henry Bernstein (1999) 'Ghana's drug economy: Some preliminary data', *Review of African Political Economy* 26 (79): 13–32; Julian Bloomer (2009) 'Using a political ecology framework to examine extra-legal livelihood strategies: A Lesotho-based case study of cultivation of and trade in cannabis', *Journal of Political Ecology* 16; Brian du Toit (1980) *Cannabis in Africa: A Survey of Its Distribution in Africa, and a Study of Cannabis Use and Users in Multiethnic South Africa*, Rotterdam: Balkema; Stephen Ellis (2009) 'West Africa's international drug trade', *African Affairs* 108 (431): 171–96; Axel Klein (1999) 'Nigeria and the drugs war', *Review of African Political Economy* 26 (79): 51–73; Laurent Laniel (1998) 'Cannabis in Lesotho: A preliminary survey,' *UNESCO: Management of*

Social Transformations Discussion Paper, no. 34; Antonio Mazzitelli (2007) 'Transnational organized crime in West Africa: The additional challenge', *International Affairs* 83 (6): 1071–90; Mark Shaw (2002) 'West African criminal networks in South and southern Africa', *African Affairs* 101(404): 291–361.

23 See, for example: www.belowthelion.co.za/time-to-decriminalise-drugs-south-african-medical-journal/ (accessed December 2011).

1 Africa's drug habit

1 Quotation from the foreword to the *World Drug Report 2010*. Report available at: www.unodc.org/unodc/en/data-and-analysis/WDR-2010.html (accessed January 2012).

2 www.nacada.go.ke/news-2/

3 Justin Willis (2006) 'Drinking crisis? Change and continuity in cultures of drinking in Sub-Saharan Africa', *African Journal of Drug and Alcohol Studies* 5 (1). Available online at: http://index medicus.afro.who.int/iah/fulltext/Pages%20from%202006vol5-2.pdf (accessed January 2012).

4 For a well-written account of the role of drugs in human society and the archaeological evidence of its antiquity, see Richard Rudgley (1993) *The Alchemy of Culture: Intoxicants in Society*, London: British Museum Press.

5 ibid., p. xii.

6 See John Philips (1983) 'African smoking and pipes', *Journal of African History* 24: 303–19. He surveys the archaeological evidence for smoking apparatus in Africa, recounting the finds of Drombowski in central Ethiopia (pp. 310–13).

7 On the early history of khat, see Shelagh Weir (1985) *Qat in Yemen: Consumption and Social Change*, London: British Museum Press, Chapter 5.

8 David Gordon (1996) 'From rituals of rapture to dependence: The political economy of Khoikhoi narcotic consumption, c.1487–1870', *South African Historical Journal* 35 (1): 62–88.

9 For early accounts of tobacco use and cultivation in Africa, see Berthold Laufer, Wilfrid Hambly and Ralph Linton (1930) *Tobacco and Its Use in Africa*, Chicago, IL: Field Museum of Natural History.

10 Francisco Thoumi (2005) 'The numbers game: Let's all guess the size of the illegal drug industry!', *Journal of Drug Issues* 35 (1): 185–200.

11 International Drug Policy Consortium (2010) *The World Drug Report 2010: A Response from the International Drug Policy Consortium*, available online at: http://idpc.net/publications/2010-world-drug-report-response-from-idpc (accessed January 2012). The IDPC publishes such a response to each WDR.

12 http://www.sahealth-info.org/admodule/sacendu.htm (accessed January 2012).

13 For a good introduction

to the pharmacological action of psychoactive substances – which also has a useful survey of sociological and psychological approaches to drug use – see: Howard Abadinsky (2001) *Drugs: An Introduction*, 4th Edn, Belmont, CA: Wadsworth.

14 Zinberg's classic work, Norman E. Zinberg (1984) *Drug, Set and Setting: The Basis for Controlled Heroin Use*, New Haven, CT: Yale University Press, has been influential in the study of drug use, urging a holistic approach that takes into account the individual drug, the 'set' or idiosyncratic psychological aspects – including mood, personal history and so forth – and the 'setting' or physical and social contexts of consumption.

15 Justin Willis (2002) *Potent Brews: A Social History of Alcohol in East Africa, 1850–1999*, Oxford: James Currey, pp. 7–8.

16 For an anthropological account of the placebo effect, see Daniel Moerman (2002) *Meaning, Medicine and the 'Placebo Effect'*, Cambridge: University Press.

17 Howard Becker (1953) 'Becoming a marihuana user', *The American Journal of Sociology* 59 (3): 235–42.

18 On *iboga*, see James Fernandez (1982) *Bwiti: An Ethnography of the Religious Imagination in Africa*, Princeton, NJ: Princeton University Press.

19 See Merid W. Aregay (1988) 'The early history of Ethiopia's coffee trade and the rise of

Shawa', *Journal of African History* 29 (1): 19–25.

20 For an account of the *buna qalla* among the Borana (an Oromo-speaking people) see Mario Aguilar (1998) *Being Oromo in Kenya*, Trenton, NJ: Africa World Press, Chapter 5.

21 Paul E. Lovejoy (2007) 'The "coffee" of the central Sudan', in Jordan Goodman, Paul E. Lovejoy and Andrew Sherratt (eds) *Consuming Habits: Global and Historical Perspectives on How Cultures Define Drugs*, London: Routledge, pp. 99–100.

22 ibid., pp. 99–102.

23 Willis (2002) *Potent Brews*.

24 Pamela Scully (1992) 'Liquor and labor in the Western Cape, 1870–1900', in J. Crush and C. Ambler (eds) *Liquor and Labor in Southern Africa*, Ohio: University Press, pp. 56–77.

25 IRIN (2009) 'South Africa: Coming to terms with the tot system's hangover', available online at: www.irinnews.org/Report/84542/SOUTH-AFRICA-Coming-to-terms-with-the-tot-system-s-hangover (accessed April 2012).

26 Emmanuel Akyeampong (1996) *Drink, Power, and Cultural Change: A Social History of Alcohol in Ghana, c.1800 to Recent Times*, Oxford: James Currey.

27 Charles Ambler and Jonathan Crush (1992) 'Alcohol in southern African labor history', in J. Crush and C. Ambler (eds) *Liquor and Labor in Southern Africa*, Ohio: University Press, pp. 3–4.

28 Lynn Schler (2002) 'Looking through a glass of beer: Alcohol in the cultural spaces of colonial Douala, 1910–1945', *International Journal of African Historical Studies* 35 (2–3): 334.

29 See, for example, the recent volume: Steven van Wolputte and Mattia Fumanti (eds) (2010) *Beer in Africa: Drinking Spaces, States and Selves*, Berlin: Lit Verlag.

30 Laufer et al., *Tobacco and Its Use in Africa*.

31 Michael Odenwald, Frank Neuner, Maggie Schauer, Thomas Elbert, Claudia Catani, Birker Lingenfelder, Harald Hinkel, Heinz Häfner and Brigitte Rockstroh (2005) 'Khat use as risk factor for psychotic disorders: A cross-sectional and case-control study in Somalia', *BMC Medicine* 3 (5). Available at: www.biomedcentral.com/1741-7015/3/5.

32 Glenice Cox and Hagen Rampes (2003) 'Adverse effects of khat: A review', *Advances in Psychiatric Treatment* 9: 456–63.

33 Regarding 'social harms' in the diaspora, see David Anderson and Neil Carrier (2011) *Khat: Social Harms and Legislation, a Literature Review*, Occasional Paper 95, UK Home Office. Available at: www.homeoffice.gov.uk/publications/science-research-statistics/research-statistics/crime-research/occ95 (accessed January 2012).

34 Peter Hansen (2009) *Governing Khat: Drugs and Democracy in Somaliland*, Danish Institute for International Studies working paper. Available at: www.diis.dk/sw86068.asp (accessed January 2012).

35 David Anderson and Neil Carrier (2009) 'Khat in colonial Kenya: A history of prohibition and control', *Journal of African History* 50 (3): 377–97.

36 Lee Cassanelli (1986) 'Qat: Changes in the production and consumption of a quasi-legal commodity in northeast Africa', in Arjun Appadurai (ed.) *The Social Life of Things: Commodities in Cultural Perspective*, Cambridge: University Press, pp. 236–60.

37 UNODC (2007) *Cannabis in Africa: An Overview*, Vienna: UNODC, p. 15.

38 UNDCP (1999) *The Drug Nexus in Africa*, Vienna: UNDCP.

39 UNODC, *World Drug Report 2010*.

40 Ted Leggett (2002) *Rainbow Vice: The Drugs and Sex Industries in the New South Africa*, London: Zed Books, p. 38.

41 For example, see ibid., p. 37, on the situation in South Africa, and Axel Klein (1999) 'Nigeria and the drugs war', *Review of African Political Economy* 26(79): 51–73.

42 Brian du Toit (1975) 'Dagga: The history and ethnographic setting of *Cannabis sativa* in southern Africa', in Vera Rubin (ed.) *Cannabis and Culture*, The Hague: Mouton De Gruyter, pp. 81–116.

43 Laurent Laniel, Oxford talk available at: http://laniel.free.fr/INDEXES/PapersIndex/CANNABIS_AFRICA_OXFORD/Cannabis_in_Africa_Oxford.htm#_ftn3.

44 Brian du Toit, 'Dagga', p. 84.

45 Johannes Fabian (2000) *Out of Our Minds*, Berkeley: University of California Press.

46 Du Toit, 'Dagga', pp. 96–7.

47 Emmanuel Akyeampong (2005) 'Diaspora and drug trafficking in West Africa: A case study of Ghana', *African Affairs* 104 (416): 429–47.

48 Axel Klein, 'Nigeria and the drugs war', p. 55.

49 ibid., p. 60.

50 Laniel, Oxford talk, Footnote 5. On cannabis use in work contexts in the Caribbean, see the work of medical anthropologist Melanie Dreher, e.g. (1983) 'Marihuana and work: Cannabis smoking on a Jamaican sugar estate', *Human Organization* 42: 1–8.

51 Drug consumption is strongly associated with insanity in Africa, an association established partly through the treatment of drug users in mental hospitals.

52 http://www.youtube.com/watch?v=aVHLqht9lew.

53 Henry Bernstein (1999) 'Ghana's drug economy: Some preliminary data', *Review of African Political Economy* 26(79): 18.

54 Savishinsky estimates that 50–60 per cent of *Baye Faal* are cannabis smokers: Neil T. Savishinsky (1994) 'The Baye Faal of Senegambia: Muslim Rastas in the Promised Land', *Africa* 64 (2): 212.

55 UNDCP, *The Drug Nexus in Africa*, p. 40.

56 Leggett, *Rainbow Vice*; Rodney Scholes (2007) 'Illegal use and in particular tik and criminal groups in the Western Cape', unpublished dissertation, University of Cape Town. Available at: www.lawspace2.lib.uct.ac.za/dspace/bitstream/2165/329/1/SCHOROD003.pdf; Jonny Steinberg (2005) 'The illicit abalone trade in South Africa', *Institute for Security Studies, Occasional Paper 105*. Available at: www.iss.co.za/pubs/papers/105/Paper105.htm (accessed January 2011).

57 Leggett, *Rainbow Vice*, p. 44.

58 ibid., p. 43.

59 ibid., pp. 46–51.

60 For details of methamphetamine's pharmacology see Abadinsky, *Drugs: An Introduction*, Chapter 5.

61 Naeelah Scott, a resident of Mitchell Plains on the Cape Flats, quoted in: Clare Kapp (2008) 'Crystal meth boom adds to South Africa's health challenges', *The Lancet* 371 (9608): 193–4.

62 Axel Klein (2008) *Drugs and the World*, London: Reaktion Books, p. 47.

63 Scholes, 'Illegal use and in particular tic'.

64 *World Drug Report 2010*.

65 Steinberg, 'The illicit abalone trade'.

66 Kapp, 'Crystal Meth boom'.

67 Andreas Plüddemann, Bronwyn Myers and Charles Parry (2009) *Fact Sheet Methamphetamine*, Medical Research Council, South Africa. Available at: www.sahealthinfo.org/admodule/

methamphetamine.pdf (accessed January 2011).

68 UNDCP, *The Drug Nexus in Africa*, p. 20.

69 Dorothy Logie (2007) 'Africans die in pain because of fears of opiate addiction', *British Medical Journal* 335(7622): 685.

70 Susan Beckerleg (1995) 'Brown sugar or Friday prayers: Youth choices and community building in coastal Kenya', *African Affairs* 94: 23–38.

71 M. Odek-Ogunde, W. Lore and F. R. Owiti (2003) 'Risky behaviours among injecting drug users in Kenya', *Proceedings of 14th International Conference on the Reduction of Drug Related Harm*, Chiang Mai, Thailand.

72 One is a video entitled 'The Invisible Man: Confessions of a Cocaine Dealer', by a video journalist called Stephen Digges, available at: www.youtube.com/watch?v=OBLBrjD2E2o (accessed January 2011); the other is a report by Kenya's Citizen TV channel on the drugs trade in Kawangware estate in Nairobi, available at: www.youtube.com/watch?v=y-n6is5UVMw (accessed January 2011).

73 Susan Beckerleg, Maggie Telfer and Gillian Lewando Hundt (2005) 'The rise of injecting drug use in east Africa: A case study from Kenya', *Harm Reduction Journal* 2 (12). Available at: www.harmreductionjournal.com/content/2/1/12.

74 ibid.

75 Sheryl McCurdy (2009) 'Drugs and gender in Tanzania', *Africa Past and Present Episode 24*, 30 March podcast. Available at: http://afripod.aodl.org/2009/03/africa-past-and-present-episode-24/ (accessed January 2012)

76 Susan Beckerleg and Gillian Hundt (2005) 'Women heroin users: Exploring the limitations of the structural violence approach', *International Journal of Drug Policy* 16: 183–90.

77 UNDCP (2000) *Rapid Situation Assessment of Drug Abuse in Nigeria*, Vienna: UNDCP, p. 3. Olabisi Odejide (1993) 'Drug abuse in Nigeria: Nature, extent, policy formation and role of Nigeria Drug Law Enforcement Agency (NDLEA)', in Isidore Obot (ed.) *Epidemiology and Control of Substance Abuse in Nigeria*, Jos, Nigeria: Center for Research and Information on Substance Abuse, p. 169.

78 Axel Klein (1994) 'Trapped in the traffick: Growing problems of drug consumption in Lagos', *Journal of Modern African Studies* 32 (4): 669.

79 ibid., p. 670.

80 ibid., pp. 672–3.

81 Leggett, *Rainbow Vice*, p. 138.

82 Klein, 'Nigeria and the drugs war', p. 55.

83 Mohamed J. U. Dahoma, Ahmed A. Salim, Reychad Abdool, Asha A. Othman, Hassan Makame, Ali S. Ali, Asha Abdalla, Said Juma, Badria Yahya, Shaka H. Shaka, Mohammed Sharif, Asha M. Seha, Mahmoud Mussa,

Omar M. Shauri, Lucy Nganga and Tabitha Kibuka (2006) 'HIV and substance use: The dual epidemics challenging Zanzibar', *African Journal of Drug and Alcohol Studies* 5 (2): 133.

84 ibid..

85 Susan Beckerleg et al., 'The rise of injecting drug use'.

86 Savanna R. Reid (2009) 'Injection drug use, unsafe medical injections, and HIV in Africa: A systematic review', *Harm Reduction Journal* 6 (24). Available at: www.harmreductionjournal.com/content/6/1/24.

87 Julian Buchanan (2004) 'Missing links? Problem drug use and social exclusion', *Probation Journal* 51 (4): 387.

88 Reid, 'Injection drug use'.

89 S. McCurdy, M. W. Ross, M. L. Williams, G. P. Kilonzo and M. T. Leshabari (2010) 'Flashblood: Blood sharing among female injecting drug users in Tanzania', *Addiction* 105 (6): 1062.

90 Paul Sendziuk (2007) 'Harm reduction and HIV-prevention among injecting drug users in Australia: An international comparison', *Canadian Bulletin of Medical History* 24 (1): 113 –29.

91 Reid, 'Injection drug use'.

92 The US President's Emergency Plan for AIDS Relief (PEP-FAR) (2010) *Comprehensive HIV Prevention for People who Inject Drugs, Revised Guidance*. Available at: www.pepfar.gov/documents/organization/144970.pdf (accessed January 2011).

93 Report by Plus News, 24 August 2010. Available at: www.reliefweb.int/rw/rwb.nsf/db900sid/MDCS-88MDES?OpenDocument (accessed January 2011).

2 Drugs and development

1 Quoted in: M. Singer (2008) 'Drugs and development: The global impact of drug use and trafficking on social and economic development', *International Journal of Drug Policy* 19: 468.

2 From the United Nations website: www.un.org/millennium goals/ (accessed January 2012).

3 Antonio Maria Costa (2008) 'Every line of cocaine means a little part of Africa dies', 9 March, *Guardian*, 'Comment is free' section online, available at: www.guardian.co.uk/commentis free/2008/mar/09/drugstrade. united nations (accessed April 2011).

4 On the 'securitization of development' in the Kenyan context, see: Jan Bachman and Jana Hönke (2010) '"Peace and security" as counterterrorism? Old and new liberal interventions and their social effects in Kenya', *African Affairs* 109 (434): 97–114.

5 Merrill Singer (2008) *Drugs and Development: The Global Impact on Sustainable Growth and Human Rights*, Long Grove, IL: Waveland Press.

6 ibid., p. 44.

7 ibid., p. 49.

8 As paraphrased on the UNODC website: www.unodc.org/unodc/en/corruption/index.html (accessed January 2012).

9 Singer, *Drugs and Development*, p. 51.

10 Report of the International Narcotics Control Board (2003), available at: www.incb.org/incb/annual_report_2003.html (accessed January 2012), p. 39.

11 Cable from Freetown US Embassy to Washington, ID no. #09FREETOWN135, 14 April 2009. Available at: www.cablegatesearch.net/cable.php?id=09FREETOWN135 (accessed January 2012)

12 Wikileaks Nairobi Cable No. 8, 'International drug trafficking ring enjoys impunity', January 2006. Available at: http://kenyastockholm.com/2010/12/09/wikileaks-releases-nairobi-cable-no-8/ (accessed January 2012).

13 For example, see the following report on drug use by ex-combatants in Liberia: www.irinnews.org/Report.aspx?ReportId=81910.

14 Neil Cooper (2001) 'Conflict goods: The challenges for peacekeeping and conflict prevention', *International Peacekeeping* 8 (3): 21–38.

15 INCB Report (2003), p. 39.

16 David Anderson and Neil Carrier (2006) '"Flowers of paradise" or "polluting the nation", contested narratives of khat consumption', in John Brewer and Frank Trentmann (eds) *Consuming Cultures, Global Perspectives: Historical Trajectories, Transnational Exchanges*, Oxford: Berg, pp. 145–66.

17 Gideon N. Gathaara (1999) *Aerial Survey of the Destruction of Mt. Kenya, Imenti and Ndare Forest Reserves*, Kenya Wildlife Service report. Available at: www.unep.org/expeditions/docs/Mt-Kenya-report_Aerial%20survey%201999.pdf (accessed January 2012).

18 Gessesse Dessie (2008) 'Khat expansion and forest decline in Wondo Genet, Ethiopia', *Geografiska Annaler* 90 (2): 187–203.

19 David Anderson, Susan Beckerleg, Degol Hailu and Axel Klein (2007) *The Khat Controversy: Stimulating the Debate on Drugs*, Oxford: Berg, p. 61.

20 Singer (2008) *Drugs and Development*, p. 83.

21 UNODC (2009), *World Drug Report 2009*, Vienna: United Nations Office on Drugs and Crime. Available at: www.unodc.org/documents/wdr/WDR_2009/WDR2009_eng_web.pdf (accessed January 2012), p. 165.

22 Singer, 'Drugs and development', p. 472. Quotation from J.-P. Grund (2004) 'Harm reduction for poppy farmers in Myanmar?', *Asian Harm Reduction Network Newsletter* 34: 1–3.

23 Julian Bloomer (2008) 'A political ecology approach to extra-legal rural livelihoods: A Lesotho-based case study of cultivation of and trade in cannabis', unpublished PhD Thesis, Trinity College, Dublin, p. 62.

24 UNODC (2007) *Cannabis in Africa: An Overview*. Available at: www.unodc.org/documents/data-and-analysis/Can_Afr_EN_09_11_07.pdf (accessed January 2012), p. 2

25 John L. Comaroff, Jean Comaroff and Deborah James (eds) (2007) *Picturing a Colonial Past: The African Photographs of Isaac Schapera*, Chicago, IL: University Press, p. 149.

26 Structural adjustment programmes were not always bad news for farmers, as, according to Gavin Williams, such policies sometimes raised prices for crops on local markets. But such gains were usually outweighed by the fall in export prices. See: Gavin Williams (1994) 'Why structural adjustment is necessary and why it doesn't work', *Review of African Political Economy* 21 (60): 214–25.

27 Pascale Perez and Laurent Laniel (2004) 'Croissance et ... croissance de l'économie du cannabis en Afrique subsaharienne (1980–2000)', *Hèrodote* 1 (112): 125.

28 UNODC (1999) *The Drug Nexus in Africa*. Available online at: www.unodc.org/pdf/report_1999-03-01_1.pdf (accessed January 2012), p. 53.

29 P.-A. Chouvy and L. Laniel (2007) 'Agricultural drug economies: Cause or alternative to intra-state conflict', *Crime, Law and Social Change* 48 (3–5): 140.

30 Henry Bernstein (1999) 'Ghana's drug economy: Some preliminary data', *Review of African Political Economy* 26(79): 13–32.

31 Julian Bloomer (2009) 'Using a political ecology framework to examine extra-legal livelihood strategies: A Lesotho-based case study of cultivation of and trade in cannabis', *Journal of Political Ecology* 16: 51.

32 2009 UN data available at: http://data.un.org/CountryProfile.aspx?crName=Lesotho (accessed January 2012).

33 Bloomer, *A Political Ecology Approach*, p. 75

34 ibid.

35 ibid., p. 61.

36 Laurent Laniel (1998) 'Cannabis in Lesotho: A Preliminary Survey', *UNESCO Management of Social Transformations discussion paper* 34. Available online at: www.unesco.org/most/dslaniel.htm (accessed May 2011).

37 ibid.

38 ibid.

39 ibid.

40 ibid.

41 Bloomer, 'Using a political ecology strategy', p. 51.

42 ibid., p. 56.

43 Thembala Kepe (2003) '*Cannabis Sativa* and rural livelihoods in South Africa: Politics of cultivation, trade and value in Pondoland', *Development Southern Africa* 20 (5): 605–615.

44 For example, see South African campaign for legalization: www.belowthelion.co.za/arguments-for-the-legalisation-of-marijuana-in-south-africa-2/.

45 Peter Gastrow (2003) 'Mind-blowing: The cannabis trade in Southern Africa', unpublished ISS paper. Available at: www.iss.co.za/uploads/CANNABIS.PDF.

46 ibid.

47 UNODC (2010) *Report of the Twentieth Meeting of Heads of*

National Drug Law Enforcement Agencies, Africa, held in Nairobi from 13 to 17 September 2010, Vienna: UNODC, p. 14. Available at: www.unodc.org/documents/ commissions/ HONLAF-2010/V1057 094_E.pdf (accessed January 2012).

48 Francisco Thoumi (2003) *Illegal Drugs, Economy and Society in the Andes*, Washington, DC: Woodrow Wilson Center Press.

49 Chouvy and Laniel, 'Agricultural drug economies', p. 142.

50 Laura Doonan (2010) 'Why my compassion for Ethiopia turned to anger', *Independent Woman*, 11 May. Available online: www.independent.ie/lifestyle/ independent-woman/why-my-compassion-for-ethiopia-turned-to-anger-2174913.html (accessed April 2011).

51 David Anderson and Neil Carrier (2009) 'Khat in colonial Kenya: A history of prohibition and control', *Journal of African History* 50(3): 377–97.

52 Paul Goldsmith (1994) 'Symbiosis and transformation in Kenya's Meru District', unpublished PhD Thesis, University of Florida.

53 Letter from J. D. Rankine (Chief Secretary) to Provincial Commissioner of Central Province, 22/1/1948, Kenya National Archives VQ/11/4.

54 Goldsmith, *Symbiosis*; Neil Carrier (2007) *Kenyan Khat: The Social Life of a Stimulant*, Leiden: Brill.

55 Paul Goldsmith (1999) 'The political economy of miraa', *East*

Africa Alternatives March/April: 15–19.

56 Goldsmith, *Symbiosis*.

57 HMRC estimates. See David Anderson and Neil Carrier (2011) *Khat: Social Harms and Legislation, a Literature Review*, Home Office Occasional Paper, no. 95.

58 Goldsmith, 'Political economy'.

59 E. Gebissa (2010) 'Crop and commodity: Economic aspects of khat production and trade', in E. Gebissa (ed.) *Taking the Place of Food: Khat in Ethiopia*, Trenton, NJ: Red Sea Press, p. 90.

60 ibid., p. 91.

61 ibid., p. 113.

62 ibid., p. 114.

63 Data from T. Tefera, L. Kirsten and S. Perret (2003) 'Market incentives, farmer's response and a policy dilemma: A case study of chat production in the eastern Ethiopian Highlands' *Agrekon* 42 (3), cited in Gebissa, 'Crop and commodity', p. 115.

64 ibid., p. 124.

65 Susan Beckerleg (2010) *Ethnic Identity and Development: Khat and Social Change in Africa*, New York: Palgrave Macmillan, p. 182.

66 Christopher Clapham (2010) 'Afterword', in Ezekiel Gebissa (ed.) *Taking the Place of Food: Khat in Ethiopia*, Trenton, NJ: Red Sea Press, p. 206.

67 Pressurop (2012) 'Netherlands bans khat', 11 January. Available at: www.presseurop.eu/ en/content/news-brief/1383001-netherlands-bans-khat (accessed January 2012).

68 Robin Room (1984) 'Alcohol and ethnography: A case of problem deflation?', *Current Anthropology* 25 (2): 173. Hunt and Barker track the impact of this critique of anthropology's approach to alcohol consumption in Geoffrey Hunt and Judith C. Barker (2001) 'Sociocultural anthropology and alcohol and drug research: Towards a unified theory', *Social Science and Medicine* 53: 165–88. They suggest that anthropology's response to focus more on 'problems' in consumption might now be accused of 'problem inflation' instead.

69 See, for example, the case of Malawi described by Harri Englund (1999) 'The self in self interest: Land, labour and temporalities in Malawi's agrarian change', *Africa* 69 (1): 139–59.

70 Shelagh Weir (1985) *Qat in Yemen: Consumption and Social Change*, London: British Museum Press.

71 Such questioning comes from all political directions, even from the World Bank. A recent working paper of the World Bank's Development Research Group criticizes strongly the impact of the war on drugs on development: Philip Keefer, Norman V. Loayza and Rodrigo R. Soares (2008) *The Development Impact of the Illegality of the Drug Trade*, World Bank Policy Research Working Paper 4543, Washington, DC: World Bank.

3 *Africa as* entrepôt

1 Quotation available on the UN website: www.un.org/News/Press/docs/2009/sc9807.doc (accessed January 2012).

2 Lagos High Court case files: Federal Government of Nigeria vs Joe Brown Akubueze, MOT Lagos Zone, Charge No CMOTN/2/94, 14 to 25 January 1994.

3 *Newswatch* (2003) 'Richest crooks', *Newswatch*, Lagos, 7 July. Available at: www.newswatchngr.com/editorial/prime/Cover/10707221119.htm (accessed January 2012).

4 Interviews with two prosecutors, Lagos, 26 and 29 July 2005.

5 Stephen Ellis (2009) 'West Africa's international drug trade', *African Affairs* 108 (431): 190.

6 INCB (1977) *Report of the International Narcotics Control Board*, Geneva: INCB, p. 22.

7 Quoted in Joseph Kirschke (2008) 'The coke coast: Cocaine and failed states in Africa', *World Politics Review* 9 September. Available at: www.worldpoliticsreview.com/articles/2629/the-coke-coast-cocaine-and-failed-states-in-africa.

8 Henry Bernstein (1999) 'Ghana's drug economy: Some preliminary data', *Review of African Political Economy* 26 (79): 30.

9 Paul Lovejoy (1980) 'Kola in the history of West Africa', *Cahiers d'Etudes Africaines* 20 (77/78): 110–14.

10 ibid., pp. 117–26.

11 Ezekiel Gebissa (2004) *Leaf of Allah: Khat and Agricultural Transformation in Harerge, Ethiopia 1875–1991*, Oxford: James Currey, pp. 76–92.

12 Neil Carrier (2005) 'The

need for speed: Contrasting time-frames in the social life of Kenyan miraa', *Africa* 75 (4): 539–58.

13 David Anderson and Neil Carrier (2009) 'Khat in colonial Kenya: A history of prohibition and control', *The Journal of African History* 50 (3): 382.

14 Paul Goldsmith (1988) 'The production and marketing of miraa in Kenya', in Robin Cohen (ed.) *Satisfying Africa's Food Needs*, London: Lynne Rienner, p. 134.

15 Neil Carrier (2007) *Kenyan Khat: The Social Life of a Stimulant*, Leiden: Brill, pp. 89–97.

16 Dimitri van den Bersselaar (2007) *The King of Drinks: Schnapps Gin from Modernity to Tradition*, Leiden: Brill, pp. 36–48.

17 Philip D. Curtin (1998) *The Rise and Fall of the Plantation Complex: Essays in Atlantic History*, 2nd edn, Cambridge: Cambridge University Press, pp. 133–9.

18 van den Bersselaar, *The King of Drinks*, pp. 56–70.

19 Justin Willis (2002) *Potent Brews: A Social History of Alcohol in East Africa, 1850–1999*, Oxford: James Currey, p. 96.

20 Simon Heap (2002) 'Living on the proceeds of a grog shop: Liquor revenue in Nigeria', in Deborah Bryceson (ed.) *Alcohol in Africa: Mixing Business, Pleasure and Politics*, Portsmouth: Heinemann, p. 144.

21 ibid., pp. 151–5.

22 van den Bersselaar, *The King of Drinks*, p. 77.

23 Anne Kelk Mager (2010) *Beer, Sociability, and Masculinity in South Africa*, Bloomington: Indiana University Press, pp. 146–50.

24 Brian du Toit (1975) 'Dagga: The history and ethnographic setting of *Cannabis sativa* in Southern Africa', in Vera Rubin (ed.) *Cannabis and Culture*, The Hague: Mouton De Gruyter, pp. 82–9.

25 James Mills (2007) 'Colonial Africa and the international politics of cannabis: Egypt, South Africa and the origins of global control', in James Mills and Patricia Barton (eds) *Drugs and Empires: Essays in Modern Imperialism and Intoxication, c.1500–c.1930*, Houndmills: Palgrave, pp. 165–72.

26 *Irish Times* (2001) 'Cannabis haul with £14m street value seized by Customs', *Irish Times*, 10 October. Available at: www.irishtimes.com/newspaper/ireland/2001/1027/01102700012.html (accessed December 2011).

27 *Mail & Guardian* (2002) 'South Africa is an international hub of the drug trade', *Mail & Guardian*, Johannesburg, 8 November. Available at: http://allafrica.com/stories/200211070391.html (accessed December 2011).

28 Antonio Costa, executive director, UNODC (2008) 'Speech at ECOWAS Summit, Praia, 2008'. Available at: www.antoniomariacosta.com/cc/index.php?option=com_content&view=article&id=353:-west-africa-under-attack-drug-trafficking-is-a-security-threat-ecowas-high-level-conference-on-drug-trafficking-as-a-security-threat-in-west-africa&catid=37:

unodc-speeches&Itemid=48 (accessed December 2011).

29 Gernot Klantschnig (2009) 'The politics of law enforcement in Nigeria: Lessons from the war on drugs', *Journal of Modern African Studies* 47 (4): 535–7.

30 J. H. Holland and Kew Royal Botanic Gardens (1908) *The Useful Plants of Nigeria*, London: H. M. Stationery Office; Steven Karch (2003) *A History of Cocaine: The Mystery of Coca Java and the Kew Plant*, London: Royal Society of Medicine, pp. 146–7; *London Times* (1882) 'Opium cultivated in Africa', *London Times*, 1 December. Available at: http://query.nytimes.com/mem/archive-free/pdf?res=F70F1FFD3E5411738DDDA80894D-A415B8284F0D3 (accessed December 2011).

31 Peter Reuter (2004) 'The political economy of drug smuggling', in M. Vellinga (ed.) *The Political Economy of the Drug Industry*, Gainesville: University Press of Florida, pp. 132–3.

32 Gernot Klantschnig (forthcoming) *Crime Drugs and the State in Africa: The Nigerian Connection*, Leiden: Brill and Republic of Letters, Appendix 1.

33 UNDCP (1998) *Supply of and Trafficking in Narcotic Drugs and Psychotropic Substances 1996*, Vienna: UNDCP, pp. 17–18.

34 Peter Gastrow (2011) *Termites at Work: Transnational Organized Crime and State Erosion in Kenya*, New York: International Peace Institute, pp. 3–4.

35 *BBC News* (2008) 'Mali cocaine haul after firefight', 4 January. Available at: www.news.bbc.co.uk/2/hi/africa/7171219.stm (accessed December 2011).

36 Mark Shaw (2002) 'West African criminal networks in South and southern Africa', *African Affairs* 101 (404): 291–361.

37 *Reuters* (2008) 'French navy in big cocaine seizure off West Africa', 31 January. Available at: http://uk.reuters.com/article/2008/01/31/uk-drugs-westafrica-idUKL3136936820080131; *BBC News* (2010) 'Gambia puts 12 on trial for drugs trafficking', 19 June. Available at: www.bbc.co.uk/news/10278734 (accessed December 2011); *ThisDay* (2006) '14.2 tons of cocaine seized in Lagos', *ThisDay* (Lagos), 10 June.

38 Liana Wyler and Nicolas Cook (2009) *Illegal Drug Trade in Africa: Trends and US Policy*, Washington DC: Congressional Research Service, p. 10; UNODC (2007) *Cocaine Trafficking in West Africa: The Threat to Stability and Development, with Special Reference to Guinea-Bissau*, Vienna: UNODC, p. 8.

39 Antonio Mazzitelli (2007) 'Transnational organized crime in West Africa: The additional challenge', *International Affairs* 83 (6): 1075–6.

40 Shaw, 'West African criminal networks', p. 309; Mazzitelli, 'Transnational organized crime', p. 1085.

41 Jean-François Bayart, Stephen Ellis, and Beatrice Hibou (1999) *The Criminalization of the*

State in Africa, Oxford: James Currey, pp. 11–12 and 29–30; Shaw, 'West African criminal networks', pp. 294–7.

42 Damian Zaitch (2002) *Trafficking Cocaine: Colombian Drug Entrepreneurs in the Netherlands*, The Hague: Kluwer, pp. 133–206.

43 ibid., pp. 133–74.

44 Shaw, 'West African criminal networks', p. 299.

45 Interview with former heroin and cocaine smuggler, Lagos, 11 October 2005.

46 Reuter, 'The political economy', pp. 136–7.

47 Ellis, 'West Africa's international drug trade', pp. 190–3; Mazzitelli, 'Transnational organized crime', pp. 1075–7.

48 *Agence France Presse* (2011) 'Gambia jails eight foreigners in billion-dollar drugs bust', 12 October.

49 Ellis, 'West Africa's international drug trade', p. 194.

50 US INL (2009) *International Narcotics Control Strategy Report 2009*, Washington, DC: US State Department; US INL (2010) *International Narcotics Control Strategy Report 2010*, Washington, DC: US State Department.

51 Wyler and Cook, *Illegal Drug Trade in Africa*, pp. 4–5; Ellis, 'West Africa's international drug trade', p. 193.

52 Wyler and Cook, *Illegal Drug Trade in Africa*, p. 5; Ellis, 'West Africa's international drug trade', p. 195; James Cockayne and Phil Williams (2009) *The Invisible Tide: Towards an International Strategy to Deal with Drug Trafficking Through West Africa*, New York: International Peace Institute, pp. 9–10.

53 Mazzitelli, 'Transnational organized crime', p. 1085.

54 Cockayne and Williams, *The Invisible Tide*, pp. 14–15.

55 Quoted in Joseph Kirschke, 'The coke coast'.

56 Peter Reuter (2010) 'Can production and trafficking of illicit drugs be reduced or only shifted?', in Philip Keefer and Norman Loayza (eds) *Innocent Bystanders: Developing Countries and the War on Drugs*, Washington, DC: World Bank, pp. 106–18.

57 UNODC, *Cocaine Trafficking in West Africa*, pp. 11–12; Reuter, 'Can production and trafficking', pp. 111–18; Mazzitelli, 'Transnational organized crime', p. 1073; Cockayne and Williams, *The Invisible Tide*, p. 13.

58 The UNODC, which has insisted on the existence of an expanding transit trade, has more recently observed a downward trend in the smuggling of heroin and cocaine through West Africa. UNODC (2009) *World Drug Report 2009*, Vienna: UNODC.

59 Emmanuel Akyeampong (2005) 'Diaspora and drug trafficking in West Africa: A case study of Ghana', *African Affairs* 104 (416): 447.

4 African states and drugs

1 Antonio Maria Costa, 'Remarks delivered at the opening of the ECOWAS High-level Conference on Drug Trafficking as

a Security Threat in West Africa', Praia, Cape Verde, 28 October 2008.

2 *New York Times* (2010) 'Africa's drug problem', *New York Times*, 11 April. Available at: www.nytimes.com/2010/04/11/magazine/11Trade-t.html (accessed January 2012).

3 Ken Menkhaus (2010) 'State failure and ungoverned space', in Mats Berdal and Achim Wennmann (eds) *Ending Wars, Consolidating Peace: Economic Perspectives*, London: Routledge, pp. 174–81.

4 Stephen Ellis (2007) *The Mask of Anarchy: The Destruction of Liberia and the Religious Dimension of an African Civil War*, 2nd edn, London: Hurst, pp. 19–20.

5 Robert Kaplan (1994) 'The coming anarchy: How scarcity, crime, overpopulation, tribalism, and disease are rapidly destroying the social fabric of our planet', *Atlantic Monthly*, February. Available at: www.theatlantic.com/magazine/archive/1994/02/the-coming-anarchy/4670/.

6 Menkhaus, 'State failure and ungoverned space', p. 173.

7 James Cockayne and Phil Williams (2009) *The Invisible Tide: Towards an International Strategy to Deal with Drug Trafficking Through West Africa*, New York: International Peace Institute, p. 13.

8 Francisco Thoumi (1995) *Political Economy and Illegal Drugs in Colombia*, Boulder, CO: Lynne Rienner, pp. 167–77; Francisco Thoumi (1999) 'The role of the state, social institutions and social capital in determining competitive advantage in illegal drugs in the Andes', *Transnational Organized Crime* 5 (1): 69–72.

9 William Reno (1998) *Warlord Politics and African States*, Boulder, CO: Lynne Rienner, pp. 1–28.

10 Jean-François Bayart, Stephen Ellis and Beatrice Hibou (1999) *The Criminalization of the State in Africa*, Oxford: James Currey, p. 16.

11 ibid., pp. 9–10.

12 Stephen Ellis (2009) 'West Africa's international drug trade', *African Affairs* 108 (431): 194–5.

13 ibid., pp. 178–82. BBC News (2009) 'Conté's son in TV drug confession', 26 February. Available at: http://news.bbc.co.uk/2/hi/africa/7913147.stm.

14 Cable from Nairobi US Embassy to Washington, ID no.#06NAIROBI72, 9 January 2006. Available at: http://wikileaks.org/cable/2006/01/06NAIROBI72.html (accessed January 2012). Cable from Maputo US Embassy to Washington, ID no. #10MAPUTO86, 28 January 2010. Available at: http://wikileaks.org/cable/2010/01/10MAPUTO86.html (accessed January 2012). Cable from Freetown US Embassy, ID no. #08FREETOWN 389, 6 August 2008. Available at: http://wikileaks.org/cable/2008/08/08FREETOWN389.html (accessed January 2012).

15 International Crisis Group (2008) *Guinea-Bissau: In Need of a State – Africa Report No 142*, Brussels: ICG, pp. 3 and 21–4.

16 UNODC (2008) *Drug Traf-*

ficking as a Security Threat in West Africa*, Vienna: UNODC, p. 1.

17 *Sunday Times* (2009) 'West Africa's new Achilles heel', *Sunday Times*, 14 June; *Observer* (2008) 'How a tiny West African country became the world's first narco state', *Observer*, Sunday 9 March. Available at: http://www.guardian.co.uk/world/2008/mar/09/drugstrade; *El País* (Madrid) (2009) 'El narcoestado', *El País*, 5 July. The photographs of Italian journalist Marco Vernaschi have had an immense impact on shaping perceptions of the state–drugs nexus in Guinea-Bissau. See his photo story in *Time* magazine: http://www.time.com/time/magazine/article/0,9171,1637719,00.html (accessed December 2011).

18 Marco Vernaschi (2010) 'The cocaine coast', *Virginia Quarterly Review*, Winter: 43–65. Available at: www.vqronline.org/articles/2010/winter/vernaschi-cocaine-coast (accessed December 2011).

19 Joshua Forrest (2003) *Lineages of State Fragility: Rural Civil Society in Guinea-Bissau*, Oxford: James Currey, pp. 1–24 and 222–32.

20 Liana Wyler and Nicolas Cook (2009) *Illegal Drug Trade in Africa: Trends and US Policy*, Washington, DC: Congressional Research Service, p. 25.

21 ibid., p. 44; UNODC, *Drug Trafficking as a Security Threat*, p. 10.

22 International Crisis Group, *Guinea-Bissau*, p. 22.

23 Wyler and Cook, *Illegal Drug Trade in Africa*, p. 5. Dirk Kohnert (2010) 'Democratization via elections in an African "narco-state"? The case of Guinea-Bissau', *German Institute of Global and Area Studies Working Papers*, No. 123, February. Available at: www.didinho.org/giga%20guine%20bissau.pdf (accessed January 2012).

24 Marie Gibert (2011) 'The securitisation of the EU's development agenda in Africa: Insights from Guinea-Bissau', in X. Kurowska and P. Pawlak (eds) *The Politics of European Security Policies*, London: Routledge, pp. 128–44.

25 US INL (2011) *International Narcotics Control Strategy Report 2011*, Washington, DC: UN Security Council (2011) *Report of the Secretary-General on Developments in Guinea-Bissau and on the Activities of the United Nations Integrated Peacebuilding Office in that Country*, New York: UN.

26 Paulo Gorjao (2010) 'Guinea-Bissau: The inescapable feeling of déjà vu', IPRIS Policy Brief, Portuguese Institute of International Relations and Security; US INL, *INCSR 2011*.

27 UN Security Council, *Report of the Secretary-General on Developments in Guinea-Bissau*.

28 US INL, *INCSR 2011*.

29 We are well aware of the 'artificial' nature of such terms as 'avoidance', 'resistance' or 'contestation' even when using such sophisticated notions as James Scott's 'hidden transcripts'

of resistance. This pattern of 'state neglect' and 'avoidance' should be seen as indicative of a spectrum of state–society relations, ranging from resistance to the state on one end to complete disengagement from the state on the other. The inherent problem of this terminology was discussed in relation to alcohol in Chapter 2 and for a detailed argument on the control resistance fallacy in alcohol studies, see the first chapter in Jonathan Crush and Charles Ambler (1992) *Liquor and Labor in Southern Africa*, Athens: Ohio University Press.

30 David Anderson and Neil Carrier (2009) 'Khat in colonial Kenya: A history of prohibition and control', *The Journal of African History* 50 (3): 378.

31 UNDP, *Human Development Report 2011*, New York: UNDP.

32 Julian Bloomer (2008) 'A political ecology approach to extra-legal rural livelihoods: A Lesotho-based case study of cultivation and trade in cannabis', unpublished PhD thesis, Trinity College Dublin, p. 112.

33 Julian Bloomer (2009) 'Using a political ecology framework to examine extra-legal livelihood strategies: A Lesotho-based case study of cultivation of and trade in cannabis', *Journal of Political Ecology* 16: 59–61.

34 ibid., p. 61.

35 James Ferguson (1996) *The Anti-politics Machine: 'Development', Depoliticization, and Bureaucratic Power in Lesotho*, Minneapolis: University of Minnesota Press.

36 US INL (2004) *INCSR 2004*, Washington, DC: US State Department.

37 INCB (2006) *Report of the INCB for 2005*, Geneva: INCB.

38 *BuaNews* (Pretoria) (2007) 'Lesotho: SA, country to ease cross-border movement of people', 20 June. Available at: www.southafrica.info/news/international/lesothoborder-220607.htm. *Farmers Weekly* (Johannesburg) (2011) 'Plight of SA farmers on Lesotho border worsening', 17 November. Available at: www.farmersweekly.co.za/index.php?p[IGcms_nodes][IGcms_nodesUID]=e4efe7edc70c189e708bd81bb5a555b4 (accessed December 2011).

39 Cable from Maseru US Embassy to Washington, ID no. #10MASERU1, 4 January 2010. Available at: http://wikileaks.org/cable/2010/01/10MASERU1.html (accessed January 2012).

40 Jean Comaroff and John Comaroff (2006) 'Criminal obsessions, after Foucault: Postcoloniality, policing and the metaphysics of disorder,' in Jean Comaroff and John Comaroff (eds) *Law and Disorder in the Postcolony*, Chicago, IL: Chicago University Press, pp. 273–88.

41 Laurent Laniel (1998) 'Cannabis in Lesotho: A preliminary survey', *UNESCO Management of Social Transformations Discussion Paper*, no. 34.

42 This part draws on Gernot Klantschnig (2009) 'The politics

of law enforcement in Nigeria: Lessons from the war on drugs', *Journal of Modern African Studies* 47 (4): 529–49.

43 John Campbell (2010) *Nigeria: Dancing on the Brink*, Lanham, MD: Rowman and Littlefield; Karl Maier (2002) *This House has Fallen: Nigeria in Crisis*, London: Penguin.

44 Abdul Raufu Mustapha (2002) 'Coping with diversity: The Nigerian state in historical perspective', in Abdi Ismail Samatar, Ahmed Samatar and Abdul Raufu Mustapha (eds) *The African State: Reconsiderations*, Portsmouth, NH: Heineman, pp. 161–9.

45 *ThisDay* (Lagos) (2010) 'Lafiaji – The triumph of justice', 8 July. Available at: http://allafrica.com/stories/201007120374.html (accessed January 2012).

46 Axel Klein (1994) 'Trapped in the traffick: Growing problems of drug consumption in Lagos', *Journal of Modern African Studies* 32 (4): 672.

47 Axel Klein (1999) 'Nigeria and the drugs war', *Review of African Political Economy* 26 (79): 60.

48 Human Rights Watch (2005) *'Rest in Pieces': Police Torture and Deaths in Custody in Nigeria*, 17 (11): 45. Available at: hwww.hrw.org/reports/2005/07/27/rest-pieces (accessed January 2012).

49 Oluwole Famuyiwa (1990) 'The new drug law and the medical profession', in Awa Kalu and Yemi Osinbajo (eds) *Narcotics: Law and Policy in Nigeria*, Lagos: Ministry of Justice; Taiwo

Adamson (1990) 'Memorandum', in Awa Kalu and Yemi Osinbajo (eds) *Narcotics: Law and Policy in Nigeria*, Lagos: Ministry of Justice; Interview with coordinator of drug advocacy NGO, Ibadan, 14 September 2007.

50 US INL, *INCSR 2011*.

51 US Congress (2009) 'Statement by Mr Johnnie Carson, Assistant Secretary of State for Africa, in US Senate Hearing on Confronting Drug-trafficking in West Africa, 23 June 2009', Washington, DC: US Congress.

52 US INL, *INCSR 2004*, p. 535.

53 Interview with coordinator of drug use treatment NGO, Lagos, 7 October 2005.

54 For a historically informed attempt to find patterns in different African states' political development more generally, see Chris Allen (1995) 'Understanding African politics', *Review of African Political Economy* 20 (65): 301–20.

55 Henry Bernstein (1999) 'Ghana's drug economy: Some preliminary data', *Review of African Political Economy* 26 (79): 23–4.

56 UNDCP (1999) *The Drug Nexus in Africa*, Vienna: UNDCP, p. 106.

57 A similar argument is made by James Ferguson in relation to the 'depoliticization of development': Ferguson, *The Anti-politics Machine*.

58 Quotation from UNODC website. Available at: www.unodc.org/westandcentralafrica/en/west-africa-coast-initiative.html (accessed January 2012).

Conclusion

1 Interview with coordinator of drug treatment NGO, Lagos, 7 October 2005.

2 Axel Klein (2000) 'Harm reduction in Nigeria: A new approach to drug control policy for a democratic government', *African Journal of Drug and Alcohol Studies* 1 (1): 53–70.

3 Joanne Csete (2012) 'Policy on illicit drugs in South Africa and Tanzania: Prospects for preventing injection-related HIV epidemics', podcast. Available at: www.veomed.com/va050661142011 (accessed January 2012).

4 ibid.

5 *The East African* (2011) 'Ill and need marijuana? Head south to Rwanda', 18 April. Available at: www.theeastafrican.co.ke/news/Ill+and+need+marijuana+Head+south+to+Rwanda/-/2558/1145978/-/5alxgv/-/index.html. J. P. de van Niekerk (2011) 'Time to decriminalise drugs?', *South African Medical Journal* 101: 79–80. For an overview of the South African decriminalization movement in the 1990s, see UNDCP (1999) *The Drug Nexus in Africa*, Vienna: UNDCP, p. 65.

6 Jack Yali (1993) 'Running a drug rehabilitation centre', in Isadore Obot (ed.) *Epidemiology and Control of Substance Abuse in Nigeria*, Jos: CRISA, pp. 162–5.

7 Moruf Adelekan and Olufemi Morakinyo (2000) *Rapid Assessment of the Treatment and Rehabilitation Facilities for Drug Dependent Persons in Nigeria*, Lagos: UNDCP.

8 For an overview of the Portuguese approach to drug control, see European Monitoring Centre for Drugs and Drug Addiction (2011) *Drug Policy Profiles: Portugal*, Lisbon: EMCDDA. Available at: www.emcdda.europa.eu/publications/drug-policy-profiles/portugal (accessed January 2012).

9 Sheryl McCurdy (2009) 'Drugs and gender in Tanzania', 30 March, podcast. Available at: http://afripod.aodl.org/tag/sheryl-mccurdy (accessed January 2012).

Bibliography

Abadinsky, H. (2001) *Drugs: An Introduction*, 4th Edn, Belmont, CA: Wadsworth.

Adamson, T. (1990) 'Memorandum', in Awa Kalu and Yemi Osinbajo (eds) *Narcotics: Law and Policy in Nigeria*, Lagos: Ministry of Justice, pp. 406–7.

Adelekan, M. and O. Morakinyo (2000) *Rapid Assessment of the Treatment and Rehabilitation Facilities for Drug Dependent Persons in Nigeria*, Lagos: United Nations Drug Control Programme.

Aguilar, M. (1998) *Being Oromo in Kenya*, Trenton, NJ: Africa World Press.

Akyeampong, E. (1996) *Drink, Power, and Cultural Change: A Social History of Alcohol in Ghana, c.1800 to Recent Times*, Oxford: James Currey.

— (2005) 'Diaspora and drug trafficking in West Africa: A case study of Ghana', *African Affairs* 104 (416): 429–47.

Allen, C. (1995) 'Understanding African politics', *Review of African Political Economy* 20 (65): 301–20.

Ambler, C. and J. Crush (1992) 'Alcohol in southern African labor history', in J. Crush and C. Ambler (eds) *Liquor and Labor in Southern Africa*, Ohio: University Press, pp. 1–55.

Anderson, D. and N. Carrier (2006) '"Flowers of paradise" or "polluting the nation": contested narratives of khat consumption', in John Brewer and Frank Trentmann (eds) *Consuming Cultures, Global Perspectives: Historical Trajectories, Transnational Exchanges*, Oxford: Berg, pp. 145–66.

— (2009) 'Khat in colonial Kenya: A history of prohibition and control', *Journal of African History* 50 (3): 377–97.

— (2011) *Khat: Social Harms and Legislation, a Literature Review*, Occasional Paper 95, UK Home Office. Available at: www.homeoffice.gov.uk/publications/science-research-statistics/research-statistics/crime-research/occ95 (accessed January 2012).

Anderson, D., S. Beckerleg, D. Hailu and A. Klein (2007) *The Khat Controversy: Stimulating the Debate on Drugs*, Oxford: Berg.

Aregay, M. (1988) 'The early history of Ethiopia's coffee trade and the rise of Shawa', *Journal of African History* 29 (1): 19–25.

Bachmann, J. and J. Hönke

(2010) '"Peace and security" as counterterrorism? Old and new liberal interventions and their social effects in Kenya', *African Affairs* 109 (434): 97–114.

Bayart, J.-F., S. Ellis and B. Hibou (1999) *The Criminalization of the State in Africa*, Oxford: James Currey.

Becker, H. (1953) 'Becoming a marihuana user', *The American Journal of Sociology* 59 (3): 235–42.

Beckerleg, S. (1995) 'Brown sugar or Friday prayers: Youth choices and community building in coastal Kenya', *African Affairs* 94: 23–38.

— (2010) *Ethnic Identity and Development: Khat and Social Change in Africa*, New York: Palgrave Macmillan.

Beckerleg, S. and G. Hundt (2005) 'Women heroin users: Exploring the limitations of the structural violence approach', *International Journal of Drug Policy* 16: 183–90.

Beckerleg, S., M. Telfer and G. Lewando Hundt (2005) 'The rise of injecting drug use in east Africa: A case study from Kenya', *Harm reduction Journal* 2 (12). Available at: www. harmreductionjournal.com/ content/2/1/12.

Bernstein, H. (1999) 'Ghana's drug economy: Some preliminary data', *Review of African Political Economy* 26(79): 13–32.

Bewley-Taylor, D. (2005) 'Emerging policy contradictions between the United Nations drug control system and the core values of the United Nations', *International Journal of Drug Policy*, 16, 427–8.

Bloomer, J. (2008) 'A political ecology approach to extra-legal rural livelihoods: A Lesotho-based case study of cultivation of and trade in cannabis', unpublished PhD Thesis, Trinity College, Dublin.

— (2009) 'Using a political ecology framework to examine extra-legal livelihood strategies: A Lesotho-based case study of cultivation of and trade in cannabis,' *Journal of Political Ecology* 16: 49–69.

Buchanan, J. (2004) 'Missing links? Problem drug use and social exclusion', *Probation Journal* 51 (4): 387–97.

Campbell, J. (2010) *Nigeria: Dancing on the Brink*, Lanham, MD: Rowman and Littlefield.

Carrier, N. (2005) 'The need for speed: Contrasting timeframes in the social life of Kenyan miraa', *Africa* 75(4): 539–58.

— (2007) *Kenyan Khat: The Social Life of a Stimulant*, Leiden: Brill.

Cassanelli, L. (1986) 'Qat: Changes in the production and consumption of a quasi-legal commodity in northeast Africa', in Arjun Appadurai (ed.) *The Social Life of Things: Commodities in Cultural Perspective*, Cambridge: University Press, pp. 236–60.

Chouvy, P.-A. and L. Laniel (2007) 'Agricultural drug economies:

Cause or alternative to intra-state conflict', *Crime, Law and Social Change* 48 (3–5): 133–50.

Clapham, C. (2010) 'Afterword', in Ezekiel Gebissa (ed.) *Taking the Place of Food: Khat in Ethiopia*, Trenton, NJ: Red Sea Press, pp. 201–7.

Cockayne, J. and P. Williams (2009) *The Invisible Tide: Towards an International Strategy to Deal with Drug Trafficking Through West Africa*, New York: International Peace Institute.

Comaroff, J. and J. Comaroff (2006) 'Criminal obsessions, after Foucault: Postcoloniality, policing and the metaphysics of disorder', in Jean Comaroff and John Comaroff (eds) *Law and Disorder in the Postcolony*, Chicago, IL: Chicago University Press, pp. 273–88.

Comaroff, J., J. Comaroff and D. James (eds) (2007) *Picturing a Colonial Past: The African Photographs of Isaac Schapera*, Chicago, IL: University Press.

Cooper, N. (2001) 'Conflict goods: The challenges for peacekeeping and conflict prevention', *International Peacekeeping* 8 (3): 21–38.

Courtwright, D. (2001) *Forces of Habit: Drugs and the Making of the Modern World*, Cambridge, MA: Harvard University Press.

Cox, G. and H. Rampes (2003) 'Adverse effects of khat: A review', *Advances in Psychiatric Treatment* 9: 456–63.

Crush, J. and C. Ambler (1992) *Liquor and Labor in Southern Africa*, Athens: Ohio University Press.

Csete, J. (2012) 'Policy on illicit drugs in South Africa and Tanzania: Prospects for preventing injection-related HIV epidemics'. Podcast available at: www.veomed.com/va050661142011 (accessed January 2012).

Curtin, P. (1998) *The Rise and Fall of the Plantation Complex: Essays in Atlantic History*, 2nd edn, Cambridge: Cambridge University Press.

Dahoma, M. J. U., A. A. Salim, R. Abdool, A. A. Othman, H. Makame, A. S. Ali, A. Abdalla, S. Juma, B. Yahya, S. H. Shaka, M. Sharif, A. M. Seha, M. Mussa, O. M. Shauri, L. Nganga and T. Kibuka (2006) 'HIV and substance use: The dual epidemics challenging Zanzibar', *African Journal of Drug and Alcohol Studies* 5 (2): 130–9.

Dessie, G. (2008) 'Khat expansion and forest decline in Wondo Genet, Ethiopia', *Geografiska Annaler* 90 (2): 187–203.

Donnelly, J. (1992) 'The United Nations and the global drug control regime', in P. H. Smith (ed.) *Drug Policy in the Americas*, Boulder, CO: Westview Press, p. 288.

Dreher, M. (1983) 'Marihuana and work: Cannabis smoking on a Jamaican sugar estate', *Human Organization* 42: 1–8.

du Toit, B. (1975) 'Dagga: The history and ethnographic

setting of *Cannabis sativa* in southern Africa', in Vera Rubin (ed.) *Cannabis and Culture*, The Hague: Mouton De Gruyter, pp. 81–116.

— (1980) *Cannabis in Africa: A Survey of Its Distribution in Africa, and a Study of Cannabis Use and Users in Multiethnic South Africa*, Rotterdam: Balkema.

Ellis, S. (2007) *The Mask of Anarchy: The Destruction of Liberia and the Religious Dimension of an African Civil War*, 2nd edn, London: Hurst.

— (2009) 'West Africa's international drug trade', *African Affairs* 108 (431): 171–96.

Englund, H. (1999) 'The self in self interest: Land, labour and temporalities in Malawi's agrarian change', *Africa* 69 (1): 139–59.

European Monitoring Centre for Drugs and Drug Addiction (2011) *Drug Policy Profiles: Portugal*, Lisbon: EMCDDA. Available at: www.emcdda. europa.eu/publications/ drug-policy-profiles/portugal (accessed January 2012).

Fabian, J. (2000) *Out of Our Minds*, Berkeley: University of California Press.

Famuyiwa, O. (1990) 'The new drug law and the medical profession', in Awa Kalu and Yemi Osinbajo (eds) *Narcotics: Law and Policy in Nigeria*, Lagos: Ministry of Justice.

Fazey, C. (2003) 'The Commission on Narcotic Drugs and the United Nations International Drug Control Programme: Politics, policies and prospect for change', *International Journal of Drug Policy* 14 (2): 155–69.

Ferguson, J. (1996) *The Anti-politics Machine: 'Development', Depoliticization, and Bureaucratic Power in Lesotho*, Minneapolis: University of Minnesota Press.

Fernandez, J. (1982) *Bwiti: An Ethnography of the Religious Imagination in Africa*, Princeton, NJ: University Press.

Forrest, J. (2003) *Lineages of State Fragility: Rural Civil Society in Guinea-Bissau*, Oxford: James Currey.

Gastrow, P. (2003) 'Mind-blowing: The cannabis trade in Southern Africa', ISS unpublished paper. Available at: www.iss. co.za/uploads/CANNABIS.PDF (accessed January 2012).

— (2011) *Termites at Work: Transnational Organized Crime and State Erosion in Kenya*, New York: International Peace Institute.

Gathaara, G. (1999) *Aerial Survey of the Destruction of Mt. Kenya, Imenti and Ndare Forest Reserves*, Kenya Wildlife Service report. Available at: www. unep.org/expeditions/docs/ Mt-Kenya-report_Aerial%20 survey%201999.pdf (accessed January 2012).

Gebissa, E. (2004) *Leaf of Allah: Khat and Agricultural Transformation in Harerge, Ethiopia 1875–1991*, Oxford: James Currey.

— (2010) 'Crop and commodity: Economic aspects of khat production and trade', in E. Gebissa (ed.) *Taking the Place of Food: Khat in Ethiopia*, Trenton, NJ: Red Sea Press, pp. 89–126.

Gibert, M. (2011) 'The securitisation of the EU's development agenda in Africa: Insights from Guinea-Bissau', in Xymena Kurowska and Patryk Pawlak (eds) *The Politics of European Security Policies*, London: Routledge, pp. 128–44.

Goldsmith, P. (1988) 'The production and marketing of miraa in Kenya', in Robin Cohen (ed.) *Satisfying Africa's Food Needs*, London: Lynne Rienner, pp. 121–52.

— (1994) 'Symbiosis and transformation in Kenya's Meru District', unpublished PhD Thesis, University of Florida.

— (1999) 'The political economy of Miraa', *East Africa Alternatives* March/April: 15–19.

Gordon, D. (1996) 'From rituals of rapture to dependence: The political economy of Khoikhoi narcotic consumption, c.1487–1870', *South African Historical Journal* 35 (1): 62–88.

Gorjao, P. (2010) 'Guinea-Bissau: The inescapable feeling of déjà vu', IPRIS Policy Brief, Portuguese Institute of International Relations and Security.

Grund, J.-P. (2004) 'Harm reduction for poppy farmers in Myanmar?', *Asian Harm Reduction Network Newsletter* 34: 1–3.

Hansen, P. (2009) *Governing Khat: Drugs and Democracy in Somaliland*, Danish Institute for International Studies working paper. Available at: www.diis.dk/sw86068.asp (accessed January 2012).

Heap, S. (2002) 'Living on the proceeds of a grog shop: Liquor revenue in Nigeria', in Deborah Bryceson (ed.) *Alcohol in Africa: Mixing Business, Pleasure and Politics*, Portsmouth: Heinemann.

Holland, J. H. and Kew Royal Botanic Gardens (1908) *The Useful Plants of Nigeria*, London: H. M. Stationery Office.

Hughes, C. and A. Stevens (2007) 'The effects of decriminalization of drug use in Portugal', *Beckley Foundation Briefing Paper* 14. Available at: http://kar.kent.ac.uk/13325/1/BFDPP_BP_14_EffectsOfDecriminalisation_EN.pdf.pdf (accessed December 2011).

Human Rights Watch (2005) *'Rest in Pieces': Police Torture and Deaths in Custody in Nigeria* 17 (11). Available at: www.hrw.org/reports/2005/07/27/rest-pieces (accessed January 2012).

Hunt, G. and J. Barker (2001) 'Socio-cultural anthropology and alcohol and drug research: Towards a unified theory', *Social Science and Medicine* 53: 165–88.

INCB (International Narcotics Control Board) (1977) *Report of the International Narcotics Control Board*, Geneva: INCB.

— (2006) *Report of the INCB for 2005*, Geneva: INCB.

International Crisis Group (2008) *Guinea-Bissau: In Need of a State – Africa Report No 142*, Brussels: International Crisis Group.

International Drug Policy Consortium (2010) *The World Drug Report 2010: A Response from the International Drug Policy Consortium*, IDCP. Available at: http://idpc.net/publications/2010-world-drug-report-response-from-idpc (accessed January 2012).

IRIN (Integrated Regional Information Networks) (2009) *South Africa: Coming to Terms with the Tot System's Hangover*, IRIN. Available at: www.irinnews.org/Report/84542/SOUTH-AFRICA-Coming-to-terms-with-the-tot-system-s-hangover (accessed April 2012).

Jelsma, M. (2003) 'Drugs in the UN system: The unwritten history of the 1998 United Nations General Assembly Special Session on Drugs', *International Journal of Drug Policy* 14 (2): 192.

Kaplan, R. (1994) 'The coming anarchy: How scarcity, crime, overpopulation, tribalism, and disease are rapidly destroying the social fabric of our planet', *Atlantic Monthly* February. Available at: www.theatlantic.com/magazine/archive/1994/02/the-coming-anarchy/4670/.

Kapp, C. (2008) 'Crystal meth boom adds to South Africa's health challenges', *The Lancet* 371 (9608): 193–4.

Karch, S. (2003) *A History of Cocaine: The Mystery of Coca Java and the Kew Plant*, London: Royal Society of Medicine.

Keefer, P., N. Loayza and R. Soares (2008) *The Development Impact of the Illegality of the Drug Trade*, World Bank Policy Research Working Paper 4543, Washington DC: World Bank.

Kepe, T. (2003) '*Cannabis Sativa* and rural livelihoods in South Africa: Politics of cultivation, trade and value in Pondoland', *Development Southern Africa* 20 (5): 605–15.

Kirschke, J. (2008) 'The coke coast: Cocaine and failed states in Africa', *World Politics Review* 9 September. Available at: www.worldpoliticsreview.com/articles/2629/the-coke-coast-cocaine-and-failed-states-in-africa.

Klantschnig, G. (2009) 'The politics of law enforcement in Nigeria: Lessons from the war on drugs', *Journal of Modern African Studies* 47 (4): 529–49.

— (forthcoming) *Crime Drugs and the State in Africa: The Nigerian Connection*, Leiden: Brill.

Klein, A. (1994) 'Trapped in the traffick: Growing problems of drug consumption in Lagos', *Journal of Modern African Studies* 32 (4): 657–77.

— (1999) 'Nigeria and the drugs war', *Review of African Political Economy* 26 (79): 51–73.

— (2000) 'Harm reduction in Nigeria: A new approach to drug control policy for a democratic government', *African Journal of Drug and Alcohol Studies* 1 (1): 53–70.

— (2008) *Drugs and the World*, London: Reaktion Books.

Kohnert, D. (2010) 'Democratization via elections in an African "narco-state"? The case of Guinea-Bissau', *German Institute of Global and Area Studies Working Papers*, No. 123, February. Available at: www.didinho.org/giga%20guine%20bissau.pdf.

Laniel, L. (1998) 'Cannabis in Lesotho: A preliminary survey', *UNESCO Management of Social Transformations Discussion Paper* 34, Paris: UNESCO.

Laufer, B., W. Hambly and R. Linton (1930) *Tobacco and Its Use in Africa*, Chicago, IL: Field Museum of Natural History.

Leggett, T. (2002) *Rainbow Vice: The Drugs and Sex Industries in the New South Africa*, London: Zed Books.

Logie, D. (2007) 'Africans die in pain because of fears of opiate addiction', *British Medical Journal* 335 (7622): 685.

Lovejoy, P. (1980) 'Kola in the history of West Africa', *Cahiers d'Etudes Africaines* 20 (77/78): 97–134.

— (2007) 'The "coffee" of the Central Sudan', in Jordan Goodman, Paul E. Lovejoy and Andrew Sherratt (eds) *Consuming Habits: Global and Historical Perspectives on How Cultures Define Drugs*, London: Routledge, pp. 98–120.

Mager, A. (2010) *Beer, Sociability, and Masculinity in South Africa*, Bloomington: Indiana University Press.

Maier, K. (2002) *This House has Fallen: Nigeria in Crisis*, London: Penguin.

Mazzitelli, A. (2007) 'Transnational organized crime in West Africa: The additional challenge', *International Affairs* 83 (6): 1071–90.

McAllister, W. (2000) *Drug Diplomacy in the Twentieth Century: An International History*, London: Routledge.

McCurdy, S. (2009) 'Drugs and gender in Tanzania', *Africa Past and Present Episode 24*, 30 March 2009, podcast. Available at: http://afripod.aodl.org/tag/sheryl-mccurdy (accessed January 2012).

McCurdy, S., M. Ross, M. Williams, G. Kilonzo and M. Leshabari (2010) 'Flashblood: Blood sharing among female injecting drug users in Tanzania', *Addiction* 105 (6): 1062–70.

Menkhaus, K. (2010) 'State failure and ungoverned space', in Mats Berdal and Achim Wennmann (eds) *Ending Wars, Consolidating Peace: Economic Perspectives*, London: Routledge, pp. 174–81.

Mills, J. (2007) 'Colonial Africa and the international politics of cannabis: Egypt, South Africa and the origins of global control', in James Mills and Patricia Barton (eds) *Drugs* and Empires: Essays in Modern Imperialism and Intoxication, c.1500–c.1930, Houndmills: Palgrave, pp. 165–84.

Moerman, D. (2002) Meaning, Medicine and the 'Placebo Effect', Cambridge: University Press.

Mustapha, A. R. (2002) 'Coping with diversity: The Nigerian state in historical perspective', in Abdi Ismail Samatar, Ahmed Samatar and Abdul Raufu Mustapha (eds) The African State: Reconsiderations, Portsmouth, NH: Heineman, pp. 149–75.

Odejide, O. (1993) 'Drug abuse in Nigeria: Nature, extent, policy formation and role of Nigeria Drug Law Enforcement Agency (NDLEA)', in Isidore Obot (ed.) Epidemiology and Control of Substance Abuse in Nigeria, Jos, Nigeria: Center for Research and Information on Substance Abuse, pp. 166–74.

Odek-Ogunde, M., W. Lore and F. R. Owiti (2003) 'Risky behaviours among injecting drug users in Kenya', in Proceedings of 14th International Conference on the Reduction of Drug Related Harm, Chiang Mai, Thailand.

Odenwald, M., F. Neuner, M. Schauer, T. Elbert, C. Catani, B. Lingenfelder, H. Hinkel, H. Häfner and B. Rockstroh (2005) 'Khat use as risk factor for psychotic disorders: A cross-sectional and case-control study in Somalia', BMC Medicine 3 (5). Available at: www.biomed central.com/1741-7015/3/5.

Perez, P. and L. Laniel (2004) 'Croissance et … croissance de l'économie du cannabis en Afrique subsaharienne (1980–2000)', Hèrodote 2004/1 (112): 122–38.

Philips, J. (1983) 'African smoking and pipes', Journal of African History 24: 303–19.

Plüddemann, A., B. Myers and C. Parry (2009) Fact Sheet Methamphetamine, Medical Research Council, South Africa. Available at: www.sahealthinfo. org/admodule/methamphetamine.pdf (accessed January 2011).

Reid, S. (2009) 'Injection drug use, unsafe medical injections, and HIV in Africa: A systematic review', Harm Reduction Journal 6 (24). Available at: www. harmreductionjournal.com/ content/6/1/24.

Reno, W. (1998) Warlord Politics and African States, Boulder, CO: Lynne Rienner.

Reuter, P. (2004) 'The political economy of drug smuggling', in M. Vellinga (ed.) The Political Economy of the Drug Industry, Gainesville: University Press of Florida, pp. 127–47.

— (2010) 'Can production and trafficking of illicit drugs be reduced or only shifted?', in Philip Keefer and Norman Loayza (eds) Innocent Bystanders: Developing Countries and the War on Drugs, Washington, DC: World Bank, pp. 95–134.

Room, R. (1984) 'Alcohol and ethnography: A case of problem

deflation?', *Current Anthropology* 25 (2): 169–91.

— (1999) 'The rhetoric of international drug control', *Substance Use & Misuse* 34 (12): 1689–707.

Rudgley, R. (1993) *The Alchemy of Culture: Intoxicants in Society*, London: British Museum Press.

Savishinsky, N. (1994) 'The Baye Faal of Senegambia: Muslim Rastas in the Promised Land', *Africa* 64 (2): 211–19.

Schler, L. (2002) 'Looking through a glass of beer: Alcohol in the cultural spaces of colonial Douala, 1910–1945', *International Journal of African Historical Studies* 35 (2–3): 315–34.

Scholes, R. (2007) 'Illegal use and in particular tik and criminal groups in the Western Cape', unpublished dissertation, University of Cape Town. Available at: www.lawspace2.lib.uct.ac.za/dspace/bitstream/2165/329/1/SCHOROD003.pdf

Scully, P. (1992) 'Liquor and labor in the Western Cape, 1870–1900', in J. Crush and C. Ambler (eds) *Liquor and Labor in Southern Africa*, Ohio: University Press, pp. 56–77.

Sendziuk, P. (2007) 'Harm reduction and HIV-prevention among injecting drug users in Australia: An international comparison', *Canadian Bulletin of Medical History* 24 (1): 113–29.

Shaw, M. (2002) 'West African criminal networks in South and southern Africa', *African Affairs* 101 (404): 291–361.

Singer, M. (2008) 'Drugs and development: The global impact of drug use and trafficking on social and economic development', *International Journal of Drug Policy* 19: 467–78.

— (2008) *Drugs and Development: The Global Impact on Sustainable Growth and Human Rights*, Long Grove, IL: Waveland Press.

Steinberg, J. (2005) 'The illicit abalone trade in South Africa', *Institute for Security Studies, Occasional Paper 105.* Available at: www.iss.co.za/pubs/papers/105/Paper105.htm (accessed January 2011).

Tefera, T., J. Kirsten and S. Perret (2003) 'Market incentives, farmer's response and a policy dilemma: A case study of chat production in the eastern Ethiopian Highlands', *Agrekon* 42 (3): 213–27.

Thoumi, F. (1995) *Political Economy and Illegal Drugs in Colombia*, Boulder, CO: Lynne Rienner.

— (1999) 'The role of the state, social institutions and social capital in determining competitive advantage in illegal drugs in the Andes', *Transnational Organized Crime* 5 (1): 67–96.

— (2003) *Illegal Drugs, Economy and Society in the Andes*, Washington, DC: Woodrow Wilson Center Press.

— (2005) 'The numbers game: Let's all guess the size of the illegal drug industry!', *Journal of Drug Issues* 35 (1): 185–200.

UNDCP (United Nations Drug

Control Programme) (1998) *Supply of and Trafficking in Narcotic Drugs and Psychotropic Substances 1996*, Vienna: UN-DCP.

— (1999) *The Drug Nexus in Africa*, Vienna: UNDCP.

— (2000) *Rapid Situation Assessment of Drug Abuse in Nigeria*, Vienna: UNDCP.

UNDP (United Nations Development Programme) (2011) *Human Development Report 2011*, New York: UNDP.

United Nations News Centre (2009) 'Human rights, harm reduction key to drug policy, UN rights chief says', 10 March. Available at: www.un.org/apps/news/story.asp?NewsID=30135&Cr=UNODC&Cr1 (accessed January 2012).

United Nations Security Council (2011) *Report of the Secretary-General on Developments in Guinea-Bissau and on the Activities of the United Nations Integrated Peacebuilding Office in that Country*, New York: United Nations.

UNODC (United Nations Office on Drugs and Crime) (2003) *Operational Priorities: Guidelines for the Medium-term*, Vienna: UNODC.

— (2007) *Cannabis in Africa: An Overview*, Vienna: UNODC.

— (2007) *Cocaine Trafficking in West Africa: The Threat to Stability and Development, with Special Reference to Guinea-Bissau*, Vienna: UNODC.

— (2008) *Drug Trafficking as a Security Threat in West Africa*, Vienna: UNODC.

— (2009) *World Drug Report 2009*, Vienna: UNODC.

— (2010) *World Drug Report 2010*, Vienna: UNODC.

— (2010) *Report of the Twentieth Meeting of Heads of National Drug Law Enforcement Agencies, Africa, held in Nairobi from 13 to 17 September 2010*, Vienna: UNODC. Available at: www.unodc.org/documents/commissions/HONLAF-2010/V1057094_E.pdf

— (2011) *World Drug Report 2011*, Vienna: UNODC.

US INL (United States Department of State: Bureau of International Narcotics and Law) (2004) *International Narcotics Control Strategy Report 2004*, Washington, DC: US State Department.

— (2009) *International Narcotics Control Strategy Report 2009*, Washington, DC: US State Department.

— (2010) *International Narcotics Control Strategy Report 2010*, Washington, DC: US State Department.

— (2011) *International Narcotics Control Strategy Report 2011*, Washington, DC: US State Department.

van den Bersselaar, D. (2007) *The King of Drinks: Schnapps Gin from Modernity to Tradition*, Leiden: Brill.

van Niekerk, J. P. de (2011) 'Time to decriminalise drugs?', *South*

African Medical Journal 101: 79–80.

van Wolputte, S. and M. Fumanti (eds) (2010) *Beer in Africa: Drinking Spaces, States and Selves*, Berlin: Lit Verlag.

Vernaschi, M. (2010) 'The cocaine coast', *Virginia Quarterly Review* Winter: 43–65. Available at: www.vqronline.org/articles/2010/winter/vernaschi-cocaine-coast (accessed December 2011).

Weir, S. (1985) *Qat in Yemen: Consumption and Social Change*, London: British Museum Press.

Williams, G. (1994) 'Why structural adjustment is necessary and why it doesn't work', *Review of African Political Economy* 21 (60): 214–25.

Willis, J. (2002) *Potent Brews: A Social History of Alcohol in East Africa, 1850–1999*, Oxford: James Currey.

— (2006) 'Drinking crisis? Change and continuity in cultures of drinking in Sub-Saharan Africa', *African Journal of Drug and Alcohol Studies* 5 (1). Available at: http://indexmedicus.afro.who.int/iah/fulltext/Pages%20from%202006vol5-2.pdf (accessed January 2012).

Wyler, L. and N. Cook (2009) *Illegal Drug Trade in Africa: Trends and US Policy*, Washington, DC: Congressional Research Service.

Yali, J. (1993) 'Running a drug rehabilitation centre', in Isidore Obot (ed.) *Epidemiology and Control of Substance Abuse in Nigeria*, Jos: CRISA, pp. 162–5.

Zaitch, D. (2002) *Trafficking Cocaine: Colombian Drug Entrepreneurs in the Netherlands*, The Hague: Kluwer.

Zinberg, N. (1984) *Drug, Set and Setting: The Basis for Controlled Heroin Use*, New Haven, CT: Yale University Press.

Bibliography

Index